# Learning PrimeFaces Extensions Development

Develop advanced frontend applications using PrimeFaces Extensions components and plugins

**Sudheer Jonna**

PUBLISHING

BIRMINGHAM - MUMBAI

# Learning PrimeFaces Extensions Development

First published: March 2014

Production Reference: 1190314

Published by Packt Publishing Ltd.
Livery Place
35 Livery Street
Birmingham B3 2PB, UK.

ISBN 978-1-78398-324-7

www.packtpub.com

Cover Image by Junaid Shah (junaidshah111@gmail.com)

# Credits

# About the Author

**Sudheer Jonna** was born in Andhra Pradesh, India, in 1987. Currently, he is working as a software engineer in Chennai, India. He has completed his Master's degree in Computer Applications from JNTU University. In the last 3 years, he has worked on providing architectural designs and built various web applications based on Struts, JSF, Spring, jQuery, and JPA technologies.

He is an experienced JSF and PrimeFaces expert. He has been working with the PrimeFaces component library since 2011. He is a committer/project member of the PrimeFaces and PrimeFaces Extensions open source projects. He is also a well-known, recognized member of the PrimeFaces community over the last few years.

Apart from the aforementioned technologies, he writes technical articles; is involved with online training, web application architectural design and development, and writing books and reviews (for Packt Publishing); and provides suggestions through forums and blogs. He is interested in the R&D of various popular JEE frameworks and many other technologies.

Sudheer shares his knowledge through GitHub (`https://github.com/sudheerj`). You can follow him on Twitter (`@SudheerJonna`) and contact him at `sudheer.jonna@gmail.com`.

I would like to thank my friends Çağatay Çivici, Oleg Varaksin, Thomas Andraschko, Siva Prasad, other extension team members, reviewers, and the Packt team for their support and great teamwork over the last few years.

A very big thank you to my parents, brother, sister, colleagues, and friends for their support in completing this book.

# About the Reviewers

**Mauricio Fenoglio** is a senior software engineer and architect living in Montevideo, Uruguay. He is a computer engineer who graduated in Informatics from The University of the Republic.

He has over 5 years of experience developing Enterprise Web Applications, especially using JEE. He is also an active contributor to the open source project, PrimeFaces Extensions. He enjoys using JSF, PrimeFaces, and the most updated web technologies.

When he isn't coding, he likes to practice kite surfing at the nearest seaside. This is the second time he has reviewed a book.

**Vineet Jain** is currently working as a project lead. He has a total of over 6 years of experience, during which he has worked on a number of projects in Java and other technologies. He has a rich experience in building applications using PrimeFaces and PrimeFaces Extensions.

**K. Siva Prasad Reddy** is a senior software engineer who resides in Hyderabad, India, and has more than 8 years of experience in developing enterprise applications with Java and JavaEE technologies. He is a Sun Certified Java Programmer and has experience in server-side technologies such as Java, JavaEE, Spring, Hibernate, MyBatis, JSF, PrimeFaces, and Web services (SOAP/REST). He is also the author of *Java Persistence with MyBatis3, Packt Publishing*, and *PrimeFaces Beginner's Guide, Packt Publishing*.

Siva usually shares the knowledge that he has acquired on his blog, www.sivalabs. in. If you want to know more about his work, you can follow him on Twitter (@sivalabs) and GitHub (https://github.com/sivaprasadreddy).

# www.PacktPub.com

## Support files, eBooks, discount offers and more

You might want to visit www.PacktPub.com for support files and downloads related to your book.

Did you know that Packt offers eBook versions of every book published, with PDF and ePub files available? You can upgrade to the eBook version at www.PacktPub.com and as a print book customer, you are entitled to a discount on the eBook copy. Get in touch with us at service@packtpub.com for more details.

At www.PacktPub.com, you can also read a collection of free technical articles, sign up for a range of free newsletters and receive exclusive discounts and offers on Packt books and eBooks.

http://PacktLib.PacktPub.com

Do you need instant solutions to your IT questions? PacktLib is Packt's online digital book library. Here, you can access, read and search across Packt's entire library of books.

## Why Subscribe?

- Fully searchable across every book published by Packt
- Copy and paste, print and bookmark content
- On demand and accessible via web browser

## Free Access for Packt account holders

If you have an account with Packt at www.PacktPub.com, you can use this to access PacktLib today and view nine entirely free books. Simply use your login credentials for immediate access.

# Table of Contents

# Preface

PrimeFaces Extensions is a light-weight, community-driven component suite, built on top of the PrimeFaces library for the enhanced JSF 2.x applications. It provides newly created, advanced, and improved components along with useful converters, validators, utility functions, and Maven plugins to make web development easier. At the time of writing this book, the latest version of PrimeFaces Extensions was 1.2.1, which works very well with PrimeFaces 4.0 and the JSF 2.x libraries.

This book will guide you through the process of setting up, configuring, and applying the PrimeFaces Extensions components in your PrimeFaces-based applications. The components and its features are explained through sample use cases and practical examples from the web application in a step-by-step procedure. This is the first book written on the PrimeFaces Extensions technology to greatly extend your PrimeFaces applications. By the end of this book, you will be able to use the enhanced Extensions components in your PrimeFaces applications.

## What this book covers

*Chapter 1, Introducing PrimeFaces Extensions*, introduces the PrimeFaces Extensions library along with its major features, setup, and configuration details by creating a simple Hello World application. This chapter also explains how to work with the PrimeFaces Extension project resources, community support, and showcase details to explore the components.

*Chapter 2, Enhanced Form and Editor Components*, introduces a JobHub application with its functional requirements and application design. After that, it explores the basic input and advanced, dynamic form components, advisory tooltip, remoteCommand, and editor components for registration-based applications.

*Chapter 3*, *Layout and Screen Blocking Components*, explains the web page structure with the layout components, Waypoint as a scroll context component to work with the infinite content loading, and the screen blocking components, such as BlockUI and Spotlight, for better user interactions in the web interface.

*Chapter 4*, *The Enriched Data Container and QR Code Components*, covers the MasterDetail component to represent the hierarchical data, cascading grid items to layout the design with the FluidGrid component, and newly added QR codes for the enterprise marketing applications.

*Chapter 5*, *Time Tracking and Scheduling Components*, explores the highly configured TimePicker component in time-valued applications, the TimeLine component for scheduling and manipulating events, and internationalization support for both these time components in multilanguage based applications.

*Chapter 6*, *Extended Data Reporting and Image Components*, explains the data reporting functionality with the exporter component, customized data reporting through the CustomExporter implementation, and image manipulation features using the Image components.

*Chapter 7*, *Common Utility Solutions, Error Handling, and Plugins*, covers the common utility components and functions to resolve problems occurring in daily development, exception handling through the AjaxErrorHandler component, and Maven resource plugins to optimize web resources in JSF applications.

*Appendix*, *Exploring Extensions Component Tags and Their Attributes*, contains the attributes for various component names. This chapter is available as a bonus chapter and can be downloaded from `http://www.packtpub.com/sites/default/files/downloads/3247OS_Appendix.pdf`.

# What you need for this book

As a reader of this book, you need to install JDK 5 or a higher version and Maven on your machine along with the compatible JSF and the PrimeFaces libraries. Optionally, you can also use software such as Eclipse IDE, debugging tools such as Firebug, and developer tools to debug your applications.

To run the customized web applications mentioned in this book, we stored the projects in GitHub, and you can pull the projects for a better and quick practical experience.

The following list of software and tools will be used in the custom web projects mentioned in this book:

- Java JDK 1.5+ from the official Oracle website (http://www.oracle.com/technetwork/java/javase/downloads/index.html)
- Mojarra Java Server Faces' latest implementation version (https://javaserverfaces.java.net/download.html)
- PrimeFaces' latest version from the PrimeFaces official site (http://www.primefaces.org/downloads.html)
- The latest PrimeFaces Extensions version (http://primefaces-extensions.github.io/)
- Eclipse from the official site (http://www.eclipse.org) or any other Java IDE
- Apache Maven build tool from the official site (http://maven.apache.org/) to work with customized projects

# Who this book is for

This book is targeted at intermediate and advanced level users (or developers) who already have prior working knowledge of PrimeFaces. Even though this book is written for experienced PrimeFaces users, it will be explained to the level of a newbie for PrimeFaces development. If you would like to enhance the PrimeFaces-based applications in an easy way, then this book is for you. Basic knowledge of JSF, PrimeFaces, and jQuery are the prerequisites required for this book.

# Conventions

In this book, we provided the headings for major topics, components, and their features in a top-to-bottom hierarchical approach. The custom web application development is explained, starting with the JobHub in action heading as follows:

# JobHub in action

Step 1

Step 2

Step 3

Also in this book, you will find a number of styles of text that distinguish between different kinds of information. Here are some examples of these styles, and an explanation of their meaning.

Code words in text, URL names, table headings and content, attribute names, filenames, commands and abbreviations, and so on are shown/highlighted as follows.

For example, the filenames and keywords are mentioned as follows:

"First we will create the `layout.xhtml` page, which will render the `HelloWorld` message in the center pane of the layout component."

A block of code is set as follows:

```
<pe:layout resizerTip="Resize Me" togglerTipClosed="Open Me"
togglerTipOpen="Close Me">
            <pe:layoutPane position="north">
                North Block
            </pe:layoutPane>
            <pe:layoutPane position="east">
                East Block
            </pe:layoutPane>
            <pe:layoutPane position="center">
                <h1>Hello, Welcome to Primefaces Extensions world</h1>
            </pe:layoutPane>
            <pe:layoutPane position="west" size="200">
                West Block
            </pe:layoutPane>
            <pe:layoutPane position="south">
                South Block
            </pe:layoutPane>
        </pe:layout>
```

Any command-line input or output is written as follows:

- The Maven run command for Oracle Mojarra is as follows:

    `mvn jetty:run`

- The Maven run command for Apache Myfaces is as follows:

    `mvn jetty:run -Pmyfaces`

**New terms** and **important words** are shown in bold. Words that you see on the screen, in menus or dialog boxes for example, appear in the text like this: "Clicking on the **TOP** button scrolls the web page to the top of the screen."

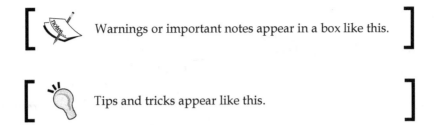

Warnings or important notes appear in a box like this.

Tips and tricks appear like this.

# Reader feedback

Feedback from our readers is always welcome. Let us know what you think about this book—what you liked or may have disliked. Reader feedback is important for us to develop titles that you really get the most out of.

To send us general feedback, simply send an e-mail to feedback@packtpub.com, and mention the book title via the subject of your message.

If there is a topic that you have expertise in and you are interested in either writing or contributing to a book, see our author guide on www.packtpub.com/authors.

# Customer support

Now that you are the proud owner of a Packt book, we have a number of things to help you to get the most from your purchase.

# Downloading the example code

You can download the example code files for all Packt books you have purchased from your account at http://www.packtpub.com. If you purchased this book elsewhere, you can visit http://www.packtpub.com/support and register to have the files e-mailed directly to you.

All the projects or source code for this book are available in the GitHub repository. You can download it from the following link:

https://github.com/sudheerj/Learning-Primefaces-Extension-Development

# Errata

Although we have taken every care to ensure the accuracy of our content, mistakes do happen. If you find a mistake in one of our books—maybe a mistake in the text or the code—we would be grateful if you would report this to us. By doing so, you can save other readers from frustration and help us improve subsequent versions of this book. If you find any errata, please report them by visiting http://www.packtpub.com/submit-errata, selecting your book, clicking on the **errata submission form** link, and entering the details of your errata. Once your errata are verified, your submission will be accepted and the errata will be uploaded on our website, or added to any list of existing errata, under the Errata section of that title. Any existing errata can be viewed by selecting your title from http://www.packtpub.com/support.

# Piracy

Piracy of copyright material on the Internet is an ongoing problem across all media. At Packt, we take the protection of our copyright and licenses very seriously. If you come across any illegal copies of our works, in any form, on the Internet, please provide us with the location address or website name immediately so that we can pursue a remedy.

Please contact us at copyright@packtpub.com with a link to the suspected pirated material.

We appreciate your help in protecting our authors, and our ability to bring you valuable content.

# Questions

You can contact us at questions@packtpub.com if you are having a problem with any aspect of the book, and we will do our best to address it.

# 1
# Introducing PrimeFaces Extensions

PrimeFaces is a leading lightweight, open source **User Interface (UI)** component library for web applications based on **JavaServer Faces (JSF)**. It provides a set of more than 100 UI components with a single JAR that requires zero configuration and no dependencies. Just as JSF (the Apache MyFaces implementation) has some extension packages, PrimeFaces has also come up with a community-driven extension and a new components set called PrimeFaces Extensions. It is a community-driven open source library that has been founded by *Thomas Andraschko* and *Oleg Varaksin*. This project aims to be a lightweight and fast JSF 2 component library in addition to PrimeFaces. It contains various components that are neither available in PrimeFaces nor in any other JSF UI library.

In this chapter, we will cover:

- An introduction to PrimeFaces Extensions and its features
- Installing and configuring PrimeFaces Extensions
- Creating a simple HelloWorld application using PrimeFaces Extensions
- Working with PrimeFaces Extensions project resources
- Community support and a showcase for PrimeFaces Extensions

# An introduction to PrimeFaces Extensions and its features

PrimeFaces Extensions is a lightweight, open source UI component library for applications based on JavaServer Faces 2.x. This project has been built on top of the PrimeFaces core library to allow users to create their own components. PrimeFaces Extensions consists of newly added components that don't exist in other JSF 2 based libraries as well as extended or improved component features missing in other popular JSF 2 libraries. Besides these components, it provides useful client behaviors, converters, validators, and other useful tools, such as a Maven plugin, for web resource optimization. It only uses standards and is highly compatible with existing JSF 2 frameworks.

Even though the earlier versions of component development with PrimeFaces started with the YUI API, in just a few days after getting negative results, the PrimeFaces team opted to go with the popular JavaScript framework **jQuery** to create their widgets and plugins. Because jQuery creates amazing widgets, custom plugins, themes, and Ajax-interactive features, considering these benefits, the PrimeFaces Extensions team also uses the jQuery framework behind the scenes to create its widgets. Hence, it is used instead of other JavaScript / UI frameworks available on the market.

The PrimeFaces Extensions library is a community-driven, open source project. This project has been licensed under Apache License Version 2 just as with many other open source projects, including the PrimeFaces library. You can use this library completely free for any open source or commercial project by following the terms and conditions of the Apache License Version 2.

PrimeFaces Extensions provides the following set of features as an extension UI component suite to the PrimeFaces core library:

- More than 20 UI components
- Support for common utility components, client behaviors, converters, and optimization tools, such as the Maven resource optimizer plugin
- Built-in Ajax support using jQuery widgets
- Zero configuration and no third-party library dependencies for majority components
- Theme support to all components
- Multibrowser support (IE8+, Chrome, Firefox, Safari, and Opera)

# Installing and configuring PrimeFaces Extensions

The PrimeFaces Extensions library comes with a single JAR and does not require any mandatory third-party libraries. To use the PrimeFaces Extensions library in any web projects, just make sure to add the compatible PrimeFaces library and any JavaServer Faces implementations, such as Oracle Mojarra or Apache MyFaces.

At the time of writing this book, the latest version of PrimeFaces Extensions is 1.2.1, which is compatible with PrimeFaces 4.0.

## Official releases

You can download the PrimeFaces Extensions library either manually or through a Maven download from the Maven central repository.

The Maven coordinates for the PrimeFaces Extensions library are as follows:

```
<dependency>
  <groupId>org.primefaces.extensions</groupId>
  <artifactId>primefaces-extensions</artifactId>
  <version>1.2.1</version>
</dependency>
```

**Downloading the example code**

You can download the example code files for all Packt books you have purchased from your account at http://www.packtpub.com. If you purchased this book elsewhere, you can visit http://www.packtpub.com/support and register to have the files e-mailed directly to you.

All the projects or source code for this book are available in the GitHub repository. You can download it from the following link:

https://github.com/sudheerj/Learning-Primefaces-Extension-Development

## Snapshot releases

If you are interested in using snapshot releases in your web project in order to get newly added components that do not exist in the recent major release or bug fixes, then add the Sonatype snapshot repository to your project configurations.

PrimeFaces Extensions uses the CloudBees platform and Jenkins as its continuous integration tool. It builds the PrimeFaces Extensions project resources on a daily basis.

 The snapshot releases are not recommended to be used in the applications directly because they are currently in the development stage due to possible bugs and are not production-ready.

Maven users should configure the following repository in the project's `pom.xml` file:

```
<repositories>
  <repository>
    <id>sonatype-oss-public</id>
    <url>https://oss.sonatype.org/content/groups/public/</url>
    <snapshots>
      <enabled>true</enabled>
    </snapshots>
  </repository>
</repositories>
```

If you are not a Maven user, then download the PrimeFaces Extensions distribution directly from the following URL:

```
https://oss.sonatype.org/content/groups/public/org/primefaces/
extensions/
```

# Mandatory dependencies

Apart from the PrimeFaces Extensions library, we need to add the compatible PrimeFaces core library, apache.commons.lang3, and any JavaServer Faces implementations, such as Oracle's Mojarra or MyFaces.

In the following table, there is a list of mandatory dependencies to use the PrimeFaces Extensions library in your project:

| Dependency | Version | Description |
| --- | --- | --- |
| JSF Runtime | 2.0, 2.1, or 2.2 | Apache MyFaces or Oracle's Mojarra |
| PrimeFaces | 4.0 | The PrimeFaces library |
| apache.commons.lang3 | 3.1 | Provides extra methods for the manipulation of its core classes |

Based on the PrimeFaces Extensions library version, you have to add the compatible JSF and PrimeFaces versions.

 The dependency for PrimeFaces is defined as a **transitive dependency**, so there is no need to include it explicitly. But it is also possible to exclude the PrimeFaces core transitive dependency with the help of the dependencyManagement tag so that you can use other versions apart from the one defined by this transitive dependency.

Proceed with the following usage of the dependencyManagement tag to exclude the transitive dependency and use the other versions of PrimeFaces:

```
<dependencyManagement>
    <dependency>
        <groupId>org.primefaces.extensions</groupId>
        <artifactId>primefaces-extensions</artifactId>
        <version>1.2.1</version>
    </dependency>
    <dependency>
        <groupId>org.primefaces</groupId>
        <artifactId>primefaces</artifactId>
        <version>4.0</version>
    </dependency>
</dependencyManagement>
```

# Optional dependencies

Based on the PrimeFaces Extensions library's features that you want to use, you may need to use some third-party libraries. The following table describes the list of optional dependencies needed to use any particular feature:

| Dependency | Version | Description |
| --- | --- | --- |
| CKEditor | 1.2.1 | To use the CKEditor component. |
| CodeMirror | 1.2.1 | To use the CodeMirror component. |
| IText | 2.1.7 | Exporter (PDF). |
| Apache POI | 3.9 | Exporter (Excel). |
| Gson | 2.2.4 | To use the layout, timeline, and jsonConverter components. |
| | | For Maven users, this library is available as a transitive dependency. |

The list of maven coordinates for the preceding optional dependencies is shown as follows:

```
<dependency>
    <groupId>org.primefaces.extensions</groupId>
    <artifactId>resources-ckeditor</artifactId>
    <version>1.2.1</version>
</dependency>
<dependency>
    <groupId>org.primefaces.extensions</groupId>
    <artifactId>resources-codemirror</artifactId>
    <version>1.2.1</version>
</dependency>
<dependency>
    <groupId>com.lowagie</groupId>
    <artifactId>itext</artifactId>
    <version>2.1.7</version>
</dependency>
<dependency>
    <groupId>org.apache.poi</groupId>
    <artifactId>poi</artifactId>
    <version>3.9</version>
</dependency>
<dependency>
    <groupId>org.apache.poi</groupId>
    <artifactId>poi-ooxml</artifactId>
    <version>3.9</version>
</dependency>
```

 Please refer to the JobHub application's pom.xml file in GitHub for the preceding configuration's details.

If you are using the iText library in your project, then don't forget to add the following exclusions in your iText Maven dependency (these APIs are not required for the PDF Exporter component):

```
<exclusions>
<exclusion>
    <groupId>bouncycastle</groupId>
    <artifactId>bcprov-jdk14</artifactId>
</exclusion>
<exclusion>
    <groupId>bouncycastle</groupId>
```

```
        <artifactId>bcmail-jdk14</artifactId>
    </exclusion>
    <exclusion>
        <groupId>org.bouncycastle</groupId>
        <artifactId>bctsp-jdk14</artifactId>
    </exclusion>
    </exclusions>
```

The following section shows the steps to install and configure PrimeFaces Extensions to your project. It has been split up into instructions for Maven users and non-Maven users.

If you are a Maven user, perform the following steps:

1.  Add the following PrimeFaces Extensions library's Maven dependency to your `pom.xml` file; it will download the library from the Maven central repository as follows:

    ```
    <dependency>
        <groupId>org.primefaces.extensions</groupId>
        <artifactId>primefaces-extensions</artifactId>
        <version>1.2.1</version>
    </dependency>
    ```

2.  Add the following PrimeFaces core Maven dependency to your `pom.xml` file; it will be downloaded to the library from the Maven central repository as follows:

    ```
    <dependency>
        <groupId>org.primefaces</groupId>
        <artifactId>primefaces</artifactId>
        <version>4.0</version>
    </dependency>
    ```

    For the projects using lower versions of the PrimeFaces library, you have to add the PrimeFaces Maven repository to the repository list in `pom.xml` as follows:

    ```
    <repository>
        <id>prime-repo</id>
        <name>Prime Repo</name>
        <url>http://repository.primefaces.org</url>
    </repository>
    ```

    The PrimeFaces core dependency is optional for Maven users because the PrimeFaces Extensions library has transitive dependency for the PrimeFaces core. This step is only required when you are going to use other PrimeFaces versions over the default PrimeFaces transitive dependency with the help of the `dependencyManagement` tag.

3. Configure the following code for either of the JSF dependencies in your project's `pom.xml` file:

```
<dependency>
    <groupId>com.sun.faces</groupId>
    <artifactId>jsf-impl</artifactId>
    <version>2.2.4</version>
    <scope>compile</scope>
</dependency>
```

The following is an equivalent block of code:

```
<dependency>
    <groupId>org.apache.myfaces.core</groupId>
    <artifactId>myfaces-impl</artifactId>
    <version>2.2</version>
    <scope>compile</scope>
</dependency>
```

If you are a non-Maven user, perform the following steps:

1. Download the PrimeFaces Extensions 1.2.1 library from the Maven central repository and add it to the classpath.
2. Download `PrimeFaces-4.0.jar` from `http://www.primefaces.org/downloads.html` and add it to the classpath.
3. Download either the Oracle Mojarra or Apache MyFaces JSF implementation from their official site and add it to the classpath.
4. Download the optional dependencies, such as POI, iText, CKEditor, and CodeMirror, and add them to the classpath based on your application requirement.

# Creating a HelloWorld application using PrimeFaces Extensions

After installing and configuring the PrimeFaces Extensions environment, we have to add the PrimeFaces Extensions `xmlns:pe="http://primefaces.org/ui/extensions"` namespace in the web page to work with the extension components. You should have at least one PF Extensions component on the XHTML page, otherwise the core JavaScript with the namespace PrimeFacesExt will not be loaded.

Let us create a simple HelloWorld application to make sure PrimeFaces Extensions has been installed and configured properly.

First, we will create the layout.xhtml page, which will render the HelloWorld message in the center pane of the layout component as shown in the following code (this layout can be used to maintain the templating mechanism of the web pages):

```
<!DOCTYPE html>
<html xmlns="http://www.w3.org/1999/xhtml"
      xmlns:f="http://java.sun.com/jsf/core"
      xmlns:h="http://java.sun.com/jsf/html"
      xmlns:ui="http://java.sun.com/jsf/facelets"
      xmlns:pe="http://primefaces.org/ui/extensions">
<f:view contentType="text/html" locale="en">
    <pe:head title="PrimeFaces Extensions HelloWorld"
      shortcutIcon="#{request.contextPath}/favicon.ico">
        <f:facet name="first">
            <meta http-equiv="Content-Type" content="text/html;
                charset=UTF-8"/>
            <meta http-equiv="pragma" content="no-cache"/>
            <meta http-equiv="cache-control" content="no-cache"/>
            <meta http-equiv="expires" content="0"/>
        </f:facet>
    </pe:head>
    <h:body>
        <pe:layout resizerTip="Resize Me" togglerTipClosed="Open Me"
          togglerTipOpen="Close Me">
            <pe:layoutPane position="north">
                North Block
            </pe:layoutPane>
            <pe:layoutPane position="east">
                East Block
            </pe:layoutPane>
            <pe:layoutPane position="center">
                <h1>Hello, Welcome to Primefaces Extensions world</h1>
            </pe:layoutPane>
            <pe:layoutPane position="west" size="200">
                West Block
            </pe:layoutPane>
            <pe:layoutPane position="south">
                South Block
            </pe:layoutPane>
        </pe:layout>
    </h:body>
</f:view>
</html>
```

In the code section, we used `pe:head` instead of the standard JSF `h:head`. There is not much difference between these two tags, but `pe:head` only provides two additional properties named `title` and `shortcutIcon`.

Just build and run the HelloWorld application using Maven as your build tool. Then make a request to the browser using the following URL path:

```
http://localhost:8080/helloworld/layout.jsf
```

After you have made the browser request, you should see something like the following screenshot:

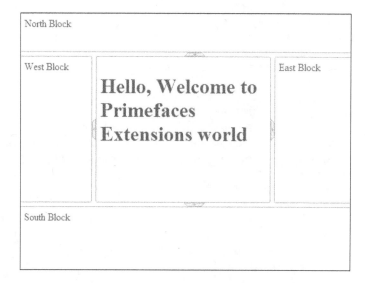

Now, the application will render or output the `helloworld` greeting message in the layout component.

# Working with PrimeFaces Extensions project resources

You can also build the PrimeFaces Extensions project resources directly from the source repositories. First, you need to clone all the PrimeFaces project resources as follows:

```
git clone git://github.com/primefaces-extensions/master-pom.git
git clone git://github.com/primefaces-extensions/core.git
```

```
git clone git://github.com/primefaces-extensions/resources-ckeditor.git
git clone git://github.com/primefaces-extensions/resources-codemirror.git
git clone git://github.com/primefaces-extensions/showcase.git
```

The `master-pom` project should be built first as it contains the required dependencies for all the PrimeFaces Extensions projects. So, we have to build the projects in the order they are cloned in. All the projects are compiled and installed in the local repository with the help of the `mvn clean install` command.

Now, we can run the showcase on the Jetty 8 server for both the implementations as follows:

- The Maven run command for Oracle Mojarra showcase is as follows:

  `mvn jetty:run`

- The Maven run command for Apache MyFaces showcase is as follows:

  `mvn jetty:run -Pmyfaces`

Access the PrimeFaces Extensions showcase components through the following localhost URL:

`http://localhost:8080/primeext-showcase/`

# Community support and a showcase for PrimeFaces Extensions

PrimeFaces Extensions has its own active forum, just like the PrimeFaces core, to discuss all the questions related to this Extensions library. Apart from this, the Extensions team provides an **Issue Tracker** for bug fixes and new component features to track or resolve these bugs for future releases. The PrimeFaces Extensions team accepts suggestions and patches in the form of pull requests.

The extensive documentation and examples of the PrimeFaces Extensions components and their features are available through the common showcase. The showcase has been deployed on the Jetty8 server for both the current JSF implementations—Mojarra and MyFaces.

Visit the following URLs to get help with PrimeFaces Extensions components and their features:

- Home page: `http://primefaces-extensions.github.io/`
- Forum URL: `http://forum.primefaces.org/viewforum.php?f=14`
- Showcase URL: `http://www.primefaces.org/showcase-ext/views/home.jsf`
- GitHub repositories: `https://github.com/primefaces-extensions/`
- Issue Tracker: `https://github.com/primefaces-extensions/primefaces-extensions.github.com/issues`

# Summary

In this chapter, you were introduced to the PrimeFaces Extensions library and its popular features. You also learned about installing and configuring the PrimeFaces Extensions suite, creating a simple HelloWorld application with a simple layout example, and working with PrimeFaces project resources.

In the next chapter, we will take a look at the form and editor components components of the PrimeFaces Extensions library, along with an introduction to a simple application named the *JobHub* application. The introduction to the JobHub application will then be used as our base to build upon in each chapter until we have finished acquiring knowledge on all the Extensions components and their features to create an enhanced PrimeFaces application.

# 2
# Enhanced Form and Editor Components

The PrimeFaces core library provides a huge variation of form components, ranging from basic InputText components to complex editor components in JSF applications. To make these form components validate against the proper results, the PrimeFaces library came up with basic message components and an advanced client-side validation framework. Even though the PrimeFaces core suite provided a wide range of form elements, the PrimeFaces Extensions library introduced new and enhanced form components that include high-level validations to make the PrimeFaces form elements and their validations more powerful.

In this chapter, we will cover the following topics:

- Introducing the JobHub application, requirements, and design
- The commonly used input components and their features
- Advisory tooltips, remoteCommand components, and their features
- Working with advanced dynamic forms and editor components

## Introducing the JobHub application, requirements, and design

In this section, we will discuss the design and functionality of the JobHub application and the implementation of the JobHub application to clearly explain the enhanced PrimeFaces Extension components.

# The JobHub application

The JobHub application is a job portal-like application where jobseekers can read job posts and apply for the jobs they are interested in; these jobs are posted by various employers all over the world.

The JobHub application provides a role-based access control security mechanism with the following three types of users:

- JobSeeker
- Employer Representative
- Administrator

To make the login process easier for the preceding roles, both the username and password values are configured as the same value. The user IDs for these roles are `jobseeker`, `employer`, and `admin` respectively.

Based on each user role, each type of user will have a different action or flow in the JobHub application. This is explained with the help of UML's use case diagram. The following use case diagram depicts the application functionalities with respect to the jobseeker, employer, and admin:

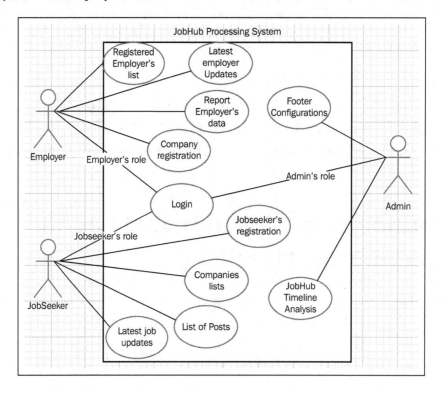

The preceding UML diagram of the JobHub application consists of three actors named **JobSeeker**, **Employer**, and **Admin**, along with the 11 common use case activities performed by all the actors. Each of the functionalities represented in the separate examples form the JobHub processing system.

The JobSeeker can perform the following actions throughout the application:

- Register with the JobHub application if the JobSeeker is new
- Log in if the JobSeeker is an existing user
- Read the latest job posts and apply for them
- View the Top Employers listed
- Check the latest updates or activities of the JobSeeker

The Employer can perform the following actions throughout the JobHub application:

- Log in process for the employer representative
- New Company/Organization registration
- Read the company standards
- View the list of companies registered with more details
- Get a report of the listed registered companies and their data
- Edit/Update the organization information
- View the latest updates of the currently logged-in employer

The Admin can perform the following actions:

- Update the site information frequently
- Analyze the JobHub reports

All the previously mentioned JobHub functionalities will be implemented and demonstrated with the help of the PrimeFaces Extensions component library; a few of the scenarios are explained with the form and editor components.

Let us start with the basic input components, their features, and how they are used in the JobHub application.

# The commonly used input components and their features

The PrimeFaces Extensions team created some basic form components that are frequently used in registration forms. These frequently used components are the InputNumber component that formats the input fields with numeric strings, the KeyFilter component for filtering the keyboard input whereas select components such as TriStateCheckbox and TriStateCheckboxMany are used for adding a new state to the select Boolean checkbox and Many checkbox components in an order.

## Understanding the InputNumber component

The InputNumber component can be used to format the input form fields with custom number strings. The main features of this component include support for currency symbols, min and max values, negative numbers, and many more rounding methods. The component development is based on the **autoNumeric jQuery plugin**.

The InputNumber component features are basically categorized into two main sections:

- Common usage
- Validations, conversions, and rounding methods

## Common usage

The InputNumber use case is used for basic common operations such as appending currency symbols on either side of the number (that is, prefix and suffix notations), custom decimal and thousand separators, minimum and maximum values, and custom decimal places.

The following XHTML code is used to create InputNumber with all possible custom options in the form of attributes:

```
<pe:inputNumber id="customInput"
  value="#{inputNumberController.value}" symbol=" $"
  symbolPosition="p"  decimalSeparator="," thousandSeparator="."
  minValue="-99.99" maxValue="99.99" decimalPlaces="4" >
```

# Validations, conversions, and rounding methods

The purpose of this use case is just like any other standard JSF and PrimeFaces input components where we can also apply different types of converters and validators to the InputNumber component. Apart from these regular features, you can also control the empty input display with different types of options such as empty, sign, and zero values. The InputNumber component is specific to Numeric types; rounded methods are a commonly used feature for InputNumber in web applications. You can use the `roundMethod` attribute of InputNumber; its default value is `Round-Half-Up Symmetric`.

The following XHTML code represents the InputNumber component with validations, conversions, and rounding method features:

```
<pe:inputNumber id="validinput" value="#{inputNumberController.value}"
  symbol="$" converter="inputNumberConverter" validatorMessage="The
  value must be less than 100.00" emptyValue="zero">
    <f:validateDoubleRange maximum="100"/>
</pe:inputNumber>
```

Apart from the regular attribute usage, you can also use widget functions such as `setValue(value)` and `getValue()`.

# JobHub in action

To learn about the InputNumber component features such as common basic usage, validations, conversions, and their rounding methods, let us navigate to the JobSeeker registration page from the login page and create the **Professional** tab under the registration wizard form. The following are the steps to do so:

1. Create XHTML code that contains common usages, validations, conversions, and rounding methods of the InputNumber component features:

```
<p:panel header="Professional Information">
<h:messages errorClass="error" />
  <h:panelGrid columns="2" columnClasses="label, value">
    <h:outputText value="Profession: *" />
    <p:inputText id="profession" required="true"
      label="Profession"
      value="#{employeeRegistration.jobseeker.profession}" />
    <h:outputText value="Experience: " />
    <pe:inputNumber value="#{employeeRegistration.jobseeker.
      experience}" required="true" minValue="0"
```

```
    maxValue="30" emptyValue="empty" symbol="yrs"
      symbolPosition="s" roundMethod="s" />
    <h:outputText value="Current Package: " />
    <pe:inputNumber value="#{employeeRegistration.jobseeker.
      currentPack}" symbol="$" emptyValue="empty" roundMethod="S"
      decimalPlaces="2" decimalSeparator="," thousandSeparator="."
      symbolPosition="p" converter="inputNumberConverter"
      converterMessage="Entered value should be Currency type"/>
    <h:outputText value="Expected Package: " />
    <pe:inputNumber required="true" label="Expected Package"
      value="#{employeeRegistration.jobseeker.expectedPack}"
      symbol="$" emptyValue="zero" roundMethod="S"
      validatorMessage="The expected package should not be more
      than 20000"
      decimalPlaces="2" decimalSeparator="," thousandSeparator="."
      symbolPosition="p" converter="inputNumberConverter"
      converterMessage="Entered value should be Currency type">
    <f:validateDoubleRange maximum="20000"/>
    </pe:inputNumber>
<h:outputText></h:outputText>
<h:outputText></h:outputText>
<h:outputText value="Preferred Interview Timings-Start: " />
<pe:timePicker value="#{employeeRegistration.jobseeker.
  interviewFromTime}" timeSeparator="-" startHours="9"
  endHours="12" startMinutes="5" endMinutes="55"
  intervalMinutes="5" showCloseButton="true"
  showDeselectButton="true" showNowButton="true" rows="2"
  showPeriod="true" style="width:70px;"
  widgetVar="customTimeWidget" label="Custom time picker" />
<h:outputText value="End:" />
<pe:timePicker value="#{employeeRegistration.jobseeker.
  interviewToTime}"
  timeSeparator="-" startHours="13" endHours="16" startMinutes="5"
  endMinutes="55" intervalMinutes="5" showCloseButton="true"
  showDeselectButton="true" showNowButton="true" rows="2"
  showPeriod="true" style="width:70px;" label="Custom time picker"
  />
  </h:panelGrid>
</p:panel>
```

The default value of the roundMethod is Round-Half-Up Symmetric(S). Other possible values are Round-Half-Up Asymmetric(A), Round-Half-Down Symmetric(S), Round-Half-Down Asymmetric(a), Round-Half-Even Bankers Rounding(B), Round Up Round-Away-From-Zero(U), Round Down Round-Toward-Zero(B), Round Up Round-Away-From-Zero(U), Round Down Round-Toward-Zero(D), Round to Ceiling Toward Positive Infinity(C), and Round to Floor Toward Negative Infinity(F).

2. Create a JSF-managed bean that declares the `JobSeeker` POJO class:

```
@ManagedBean
@ViewScoped
public class EmployeeRegistration implements Serializable {
    private static final long serialVersionUID = 1L;
  private JobSeeker jobseeker = new JobSeeker();
  //getters and setters


}
```

3. Create a `JobSeeker.java` POJO class that backs up the InputNumber fields:

```
public class JobSeeker implements Serializable {
    private String profession;
    private Double experience=new Double(0);
    private Currency currentPack;
    private Currency expectedPack;
    public JobSeeker() {
    currentPack=new Currency();
    expectedPack=new Currency();
}
  //getters and setters
}
```

4. Run the application and navigate to the following browser URL:

    `http://localhost:8080/jobhub/views/employeeRegistration.xhtml`

Now you should be able to see the following **Professional** tab displayed in the registration form:

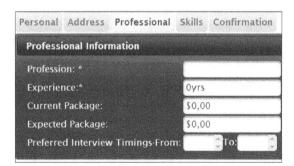

# Exploring the KeyFilter component to restrict input data

On a form-based screen, you need to restrict the input on specific input components based on the component's nature and functionality. Instead of approaching plain JavaScript with regularExpressions, the Extensions team provided the KeyFilter component to filter the keyboard input. It is not a standalone component and always depends on the input components by referring through the `for` attribute.

You can use KeyFilter in three ways; they are explained in the following sections.

## Predefined mask values

The KeyFilter use case allows built-in mask values using the `mask` property.

The following XHTML code allows `keyFilter` with the predefined mask values that refer to the input component:

```
<h:inputText id="number" value="#{keyFilterController.value}"/>
<pe:keyFilter for="number" mask="num"/>
```

Now the input component only allows numeric type of data.

## regularExpressions

The regularExpressions use case allows JavaScript regular expressions with the help of the `regEx` property.

The following XHTML code is used to apply keyFiter with regularExpressions on the input component:

```
<h:inputText id="text" value="#{keyFilterController.value}">
        <pe:keyFilter regEx="/[XYZ]/i"/>
</h:inputText>
```

Now the input component only allows the "x", "y", and "z" characters, irrespective of their case, to enter input.

## testFunction

The testFunction use case provides JavaScript code or functions that filter the input.

The following XHTML code is used to filter the companies that start with the character "C" (using KeyFilter):

```
<p:autoComplete id="autoComplete" value="#{autoCompleteController.
  value}" completeMethod="#{autoCompleteController.complete}" />
<pe:keyFilter for="autoComplete" testFunction="return c == 'C';"/>
```

You can see that `autoComplete` only allows the characters that start with "C".

> The following list shows the predefined mask values and their respective regularExpressions:
> alpha /[a-z_]/i
> alphanum /[a-z0-9_]/i
> pint /[\d]/
> int /[\d\-]/
> pnum /[\d\.]/
> num /[\d\-\.]/
> email /[a-z0-9_\.\-@]/i
> money /[\d\.\s,]
> hex /[0-9a-f]/i

# JobHub in action

Let us navigate to the JobSeeker registration page from the login page and then apply KeyFilter to all the form components under the **Personal** tab; the following are the steps to do so:

1. Create the following XHTML code that contains the various KeyFilter components applied on input and select components:

```
<p:panel header="Personal Details">
  <h:messages errorClass="error" />
  <h:panelGrid columns="2" columnClasses="label, value">
  <h:outputText value="Firstname: *" />
  <p:inputText id="firstname" required="true" label="Firstname"
    title="Please enter firstname" value="#{employeeRegistration.
    jobseeker.firstname}" />
  <h:outputText value="Lastname: *" />
  <p:inputText id="lastname" required="true" label="Lastname"
    title="Please enter firstname" value="#{employeeRegistration.
    jobseeker.lastname}" />
  <h:outputText value="Age: * " title="Please enter Age" />
  <p:inputText id="age" required="true" label="Age"
```

```
      value="#{employeeRegistration.jobseeker.age}" />
      <h:outputText value="Sex: " title="Please enter Sex" />
  <p:inputText id="sex" value="#{employeeRegistration.jobseeker.
    sex}" />
  <h:outputText value="MaritalStatus: " title="Please enter
    MaritalStatus" />
      <p:inputText id="status" value="#{employeeRegistration.
        jobseeker.maritalStatus}" />
      <h:outputText value="Skip to last: " />
      <h:selectBooleanCheckbox value="#{employeeRegistration.skip}" />
      </h:panelGrid>
      <pe:keyFilter for="firstname" mask="alphanum" />
      <pe:keyFilter for="lastname" regEx="/[a-z0-9_]/i" />
      <pe:keyFilter for="age" mask="num" />
      <pe:keyFilter for="sex" mask="alpha" />
      <pe:keyFilter for="status" mask="alpha" />
  </p:panel>
```

2. Create the following JSF-managed bean that holds the `JobSeeker` POJO class:

```
@ManagedBean
@ViewScoped
public class EmployeeRegistration implements Serializable {
          private static final long serialVersionUID = 1L;
    private JobSeeker jobseeker = new JobSeeker();
//getters and setters
}
```

3. Update the `JobSeeker` POJO class that holds the **Personal** tab properties, such as `firstname`, `lastname`, `age`, `sex`, and `maritalStatus`.

4. Run the application and navigate to the following browser URL:
   `http://localhost:8080/jobhub/views/employeeRegistration.xhtml`

Now you can see the following **Personal** tab displayed; this tab restricts the specified inputs in a registration form:

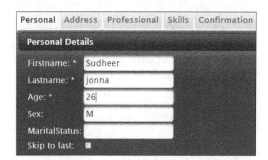

# TriStateCheckbox and TriStateManyCheckbox

Both the TriStateCheckbox and TriStateManyCheckbox components provide a new state to the standard SelectBooleanCheckbox and SelectManyBooleanCheckbox components respectively. Each state is mapped to the 0, 1, and 2 string values.

TriStateCheckbox can be customized using the title, custom icons for three states, and item label features. Just as with any other standard input component, you can apply the Ajax behavior listeners to this component as well.

The following XHTML code represents the TriStateCheckbox; it allows a new state for the existing SelectBooleanCheckbox:

```
<pe:triStateCheckbox value="#{triStateCheckBoxController.value}"
  stateTwoIcon="ui-icon-plus"  stateThreeIcon="ui-icon-minus"
    itemLabel="Item  Label">
  <p:ajax update="messages" listener="#{triStateCheckBoxController.
  addMessage}"/>
</pe:triStateCheckbox>
```

The TriStateManyCheckbox contains all the features of TriStateCheckbox (shown in the preceding code) and additionally supports various converters and validators.

The following XHTML code creates the triStateManyCheckbox with the new state to the existing SelectManyCheckbox:

```
<pe:triStateManyCheckbox id="tristatemany"
  value="#{triSateManyCheckBoxController.selectedVaule}"
  stateOneIcon="ui-icon-home"  stateTwoIcon="ui-icon-heart"
  stateThreeIcon="ui-icon-star" validatorMessage="State 0 is not
  allowed">
 <f:converter converterId="triStateManyCheckboxConverter"/>
    <p:ajax update="growl" listener="#{triSateManyCheckBoxController.
      addMessage}"/>
</pe:triStateManyCheckbox>
```

You can also find the converters that are applied to this component just as with any other input component.

# JobHub in action

Let us navigate to the registration page's **Skills** tab and add the components that choose different technologies and frameworks; the following are the steps to do so:

1. Create the following XHTML code that contains the TriStateCheckbox and TriStateManyCheckbox components with their various features under the **Skills** tab of a wizard form:

```
<p:panel header="Skills Information">
<h:messages errorClass="error" />
   <h:panelGrid columns="2" columnClasses="label, value">
       <h:outputText value="Frameworks Expertise:" />
<pe:triStateManyCheckbox id="TriBasic"
  value="#{employeeRegistration.selectedFrameworkOptions}"
  layout="pageDirection" stateOneTitle="not matter"
  stateTwoTitle="love it" stateThreeTitle="dislikes">
<f:selectItems value="#{employeeRegistration.allFrameworkOptions}"
  />
  </pe:triStateManyCheckbox>
  <h:outputText value="Database Expertise:" />
  <pe:triStateManyCheckbox id="TriAjax"
    value="#{employeeRegistration.selectedDBOptions}"
    stateOneIcon="ui-icon-home" stateTwoIcon="ui-icon-heart"
    stateThreeIcon="ui-icon-star" tabindex="2">
  <f:selectItem itemLabel="Oracle" itemValue="Oracle" />
  <f:selectItem itemLabel="MySQL" itemValue="MySQL" />
  <f:selectItem itemLabel="SQLServer" itemValue="SQL Server" />
  </pe:triStateManyCheckbox>
  <h:outputText value="Overall Expertise:" />
  <pe:triStateCheckbox value="#{employeeRegistration.avgrating}"
    />
  </h:panelGrid>
</p:panel>
```

2. Create the following JSF-managed bean that holds the **Skills** tab's backing bean properties:

```
@ManagedBean
@ViewScoped
public class EmployeeRegistration implements Serializable {
private Map<String, String> selectedFrameworkOptions;
   private Map<String, String> selectedDBOptions;
   private Map<String, String> allFrameworkOptions;
   private String avgrating;
   @PostConstruct
```

```
public void init() {
    allFrameworkOptions = new HashMap<String, String>();
    allFrameworkOptions.put("Label for JSF", "JSF");
    allFrameworkOptions.put("Label for Spring", "Spring");
    allFrameworkOptions.put("Label for Struts", "Struts");
    // default will created with state=1
    selectedFrameworkOptions = new HashMap<String, String>();
    selectedFrameworkOptions.put("JSF", "1");
    selectedDBOptions = new HashMap<String, String>();
    selectedDBOptions.put("Oracle", "1");
    selectedDBOptions.put("MySQL", "1");
    selectedDBOptions.put("SQLServer", "2");
    avgrating = "1";
}
    //getters and setters
}
```

3. Run the application and navigate to the following browser URL:
   `http://localhost:8080/jobhub/views/employeeRegistration.xhtml`

Now you can see the **Skills** tab as shown in the following screenshot with the TriState components displayed in the registration form:

You can see both the TriStateCheckbox and TriStateManyCheckbox components defined using custom icons.

# Advisory tooltips, remoteCommand components, and their features

The advisory tooltips and remoteCommand components work as helper components for other input components.

# Tooltips

Tooltips provide advisory or additional information about a particular component used in JSF-based applications. This advisory information can prove helpful before you enter valid input data or perform any operation, and also for displaying a validation message after the validation has failed on an input component.

Tooltips work as speech bubble tips and provide highly configurable features such as customized tooltips in the form of customized skinning and effects, global and global limited tooltips, shared, and mouse-tracking features.

## Customized tooltips and mouse tracking

There are many customization options such as positioning, delays, events, and effects that are available for the tooltip component. This shows an advantage over the standard JSF tooltips provided by the component `title` attribute.

The following XHTML code represents the `tooltip` component with custom events, effects, and positions:

```
<pe:tooltip for="focus" showEvent="focus" hideEvent="blur"
  showEffect="fadeIn" hideEffect="fadeIn" myPosition="left center"
  atPosition="right center">
  <p:graphicImage value="/resources/images/logo.png"/>
</pe:tooltip>
```

You can also define the tooltip position according to the mouse-tracking path on the web page. The following XHTML code creates the tooltip component with the mouse-tracking feature enabled:

```
<pe:tooltip for="mousearea" value="Tooltip position depends on current
  mouse position"  mouseTracking="true" adjustX="10" adjustY="10"/>
```

You can see that the tooltip position changes according to the mouse movements.

## Global tooltips and shared tooltips

To optimize the tooltip behavior from a single component base to multiple components or targets, global and shared tooltips prove to be very helpful.

### Global tooltips

By taking advantage of the JSF component's `title` attribute, the global mode allows a single component to work for multiple target components on the web page. This feature not only reduces the code size from multiple tooltips to a single global tooltip, but also survives the Ajax updates.

The following XHTML code creates a tooltip component globally for all the input components on the page:

```
<p:inputText title="Enter User Name"/>
<p:password title="Enter Password"/>
<pe:tooltip global="true"/>
```

By default, the `global` property is disabled, and you can reduce multiple tooltips by enabling it.

## Global limited tooltips

The global limited tooltips feature is a little different from global tooltips. Instead of applying a single global tooltip to all the components available on a page, you can supply it to a specific group of components. The best case scenario for this feature is applying the tooltips to components that didn't pass validation. In this case, the `for` attribute refers to jQuery or PrimeFaces selectors.

The following XHTML code creates global limited tooltips based on error style classes:

```
<pe:tooltip global="true" value="Please enter valid values" for="@
(.ui-state-error)"/>
```

You can see how the tooltip referred the `.ui-state-error` style selector using the `for` attribute.

## Shared tooltips

The shared tooltips feature is a little different from the global limited tooltips purpose. In this case, the tooltip is shared between multiple targets. You have to provide the jQuery or PrimeFaces selectors that group similar targets and apply the shared or common behavior through the `shared="true"` attribute. The best example is applying the tooltips for each `datatable` filter field.

The following XHTML code represents the shared tooltip features for the dataTable component:

```
<pe:tooltip value="Type any value to filter datatable" for="@
(#sharedTooltipTable th .ui-column-filter)" shared="true"/>
```

You can see the tooltip message is applied to all the filters of the `sharedTooltipTable` component.

# The JavaScript widget functions and the autoShown mode

You can control the tooltip behavior over the default normal behavior with the help of widget functions such as `show()`, `hide()`, `reposition()`, and `destroy()`. Apart from these widget functions, the `autoShown` property enables automatic tooltips to appear when the page loads. The position of an auto shown tooltip adjusts according to the window resize operations as well.

The following XHTML code explains the usage of widget functions and the `autoShown` mode:

```
<p:inputText id="text" title="Enter some value"/>
<pe:tooltip for="text" value="Tooltips can be controlled through the
  widget functions" autoShow="true" widgetVar="tooltip"/>
<p:commandButton value="Hide" type="button" onclick="PF('tooltip').
  hide();"/>
      <p:commandButton value="Show" type="button"
        onclick="PF('tooltip').show();"/>
<p:commandButton value="Reposition" type="button"
  onclick="PF('tooltip').reposition();"/>
<p:commandButton value="Destroy" type="button" onclick="PF('tooltip').
  destroy();">
```

As per the preceding code, you can control the tooltip behavior using widget functions easily.

# JobHub in action

Let us apply the global limited feature to provide form validations with the help of a tooltip component instead of using the separate message component from the standard JSF or PrimeFaces components:

1. Here we will just create XHTML code that contains the global limited tooltip component and form elements with conditional based title values in the **Personal** tab of the JobSeeker registration wizard:

```
<h:panelGrid columns="2" columnClasses="label, value"
styleClass="grid">
  <h:outputText value="Firstname: *" />
  <p:inputText id="firstname" required="true" label="Firstname"
   title="#{component.valid? 'Please enter firstname':'Firstname
     cannot be empty'}"
   value="#{employeeRegistration.jobseeker.firstname}" />
  <h:outputText value="Lastname: *" />
```

```
<p:inputText id="lastname" required="true" label="Lastname"
  title="#{component.valid? 'Please enter lastname':'Lastname
    cannot be empty'}"
  value="#{employeeRegistration.jobseeker.lastname}" />

<h:outputText value="Age: * " />
<p:inputText id="age" required="true" label="Age"
  title="#{component.valid? 'Please enter Age':'Age cannot be
    empty'}" value="#{employeeRegistration.jobseeker.age}" />
<h:outputText value="Sex: " title="Please enter Sex" />
<p:inputText id="sex" value="#{employeeRegistration.jobseeker.
  sex}" />
<h:outputText value="MaritalStatus: " title="Please enter
  MaritalStatus" />
<p:inputText id="status" value="#{employeeRegistration.
  jobseeker.maritalStatus}" />
<h:outputText value="Skip to last: " />
<h:selectBooleanCheckbox value="#{employeeRegistration.skip}" />
</h:panelGrid>
  <pe:tooltip global="true" myPosition="left center" for="@(.ui-
    state-error)"
  atPosition="right center" />
```

2. Run the application and navigate to the following browser URL:
   `http://localhost:8080/jobhub/views/employeeRegistration.xhtml`

Click on the **Next** button without entering any values. Now you are able to see the tooltip validations for the **Personal** tab fields displayed in the registration form as shown in the following screenshot:

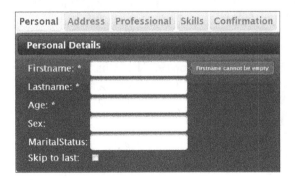

# RemoteCommand

The client-side script triggers the command remotely for executing the backing bean methods and updates the components through partial page rendering.

Command actions trigger the remote command by executing the backing bean methods and update the other parts of the page. The most common example is to load a part of the page lazily on demand.

The following XHTML code creates the `remoteCommand` component for invoking the bean property; `old` executes the JavaScript code dynamically and `new` updates the other parts of the page in the screen:

```
<p:commandButton value="Load" type="button" onclick="lazyload()"/>
<pe:remoteCommand name="lazyload" update="lazypanel">
    <f:setPropertyActionListener value="#{true}"
      target="#{requestScope.shouldRender}" />
</pe:remoteCommand>
<p:outputPanel id="lazypanel" layout="block">
    <h:outputText  value="This part of page is lazily loaded on demand
      using a RemoteCommand"  rendered="#{requestScope.shouldRender}"
      />
</p:outputPanel>
```

The preceding code explains how `remoteCommand` lazily loads the content on demand.

# AssignableParam

To assign the JavaScript parameters to a managed bean property, `remoteCommand` can take the help of the assignableParam component. It describes the name of the parameter and the EL expression represents the setter of the Java bean property. You can use the standard JSF converters for all types of conversions, whereas the Extensions JSON converter is used for JSON to class type conversions.

The following XHTML code represents how `remoteCommand` is used to assign JavaScript parameters to the bean property:

```
<pe:remoteCommand id="applyDataCommand" name="applyData"
  update="subject date circle"  actionListener="#{remoteCommandControl
  ler.parametersAssigned}">
    <pe:assignableParam name="subject" assignTo="#{remoteCommandContro
      ller.subject}"/>
    <pe:assignableParam name="date" assignTo="#{remoteCommandControll
      er.date}">
        <f:convertDateTime type="both" dateStyle="short" locale="en"/>
```

```
      </pe:assignableParam>
      <pe:assignableParam name="circle" assignTo="#{remoteCommandContro
        ller.circle}">
          <pe:convertJson />
      </pe:assignableParam>
  </pe:remoteCommand>
  <p:commandButton value="Apply Data" type="button"
    onclick="applyData('hello extension user', '14/1/14 02:30:11 PM',
    JSON.stringify(circle))" />
  //Javascript code
  <script type="text/javascript">
      circle = {
          radius: 50,
          backgroundColor: "#FF0000",
          borderColor: "#DDDDDD",
          scaleFactor: 1.2
      };
  </script>
```

As you can see, we used `assignableParam` as the child tag for `remoteCommand` to assign JavaScript parameters to the bean property.

# MethodParam

To call a Java method with arguments remotely from the client-side JavaScript, `remoteCommand` can take the help of the methodParam and methodSignature components. The methodParam component specifies the name of the parameter whereas methodSignature specifies the comma separated list (,) of fully qualified primitive types or class names. The parameter types should match the passed parameters in the order that they are defined in.

The following XHTML code shows how to call a Java method (with arguments) with `remoteCommand` using the methodParam and methodSignature components:

```
  <pe:remoteCommand id="applyDataCommand" name="applyData" actionListene
    r="#{remoteCommandController.printMethodParams}">
      <pe:methodSignature parameters="java.lang.String, java.util.Date,
        org.primefaces.extensions.projectname.model.Circle" />
      <pe:methodParam name="subject"/>
      <pe:methodParam name="date">
          <f:convertDateTime type="both" dateStyle="short" locale="en"/>
      </pe:methodParam>
      <pe:methodParam name="circle">
          <pe:convertJson />
      </pe:methodParam>
  </pe:remoteCommand>
```

```
//Javascript code
<script type="text/javascript">
    circle = {
        radius: 30,
        backgroundColor: "#00FF00",
        borderColor: "#EE00DD",
        scaleFactor: 1.9
    };
</script>
```

You can see that the preceding remoteCommand component takes the help of methodParam to accept the JavaScript parameters and methodSignature to match the Java method.

# JobHub in action

Let us apply the assignable Param's feature of the remote command component in order to display the company standards; the following are the steps to do so:

1. Create the XHTML code consisting of the remoteCommand component by supporting the assignableParam feature:

```
<p:panel>
<f:facet name="header">
Click on the following buttons to know about CMMI level standards
</f:facet>
<pe:remoteCommand id="applyDataCommand" name="applyData"
  process="@this" update="focus result standards">
  <pe:assignableParam name="focus" assignTo="#{employerDetailsCont
    roller.focus}" />
  <pe:assignableParam name="result" assignTo="#{employerDetailsCon
    troller.result}" />
  <pe:assignableParam name="standards" assignTo="#{employerDetails
    Controller.standards}">
  <pe:convertJson />
  </pe:assignableParam>
</pe:remoteCommand>
<script type="text/javascript">
cmmi3 = {
years : 5,
employees : "2k",
revenue:"10mil"
};
cmmi5 = {
years : 10,
employees : "5k",
```

```
revenue:"90mil",
};
</script>
<h:outputLabel for="focus" value="Focus: " />
<h:outputText id="focus" value="#{employerDetailsController.
focus}" />
<br />
<h:outputLabel for="result" value="Result: " />
<h:outputText id="result" value="#{employerDetailsController.
result}" />
<br />
<h:outputLabel for="standards" value="Standards: " />
<h:outputText id="standards"
value="years:#{employerDetailsController.standards.years} - employ
ees:#{employerDetailsController.standards.employees} - revenue:#{e
mployerDetailsController.standards.revenue}" />

<p:commandButton value="CMMI3" type="button"
onclick="applyData('Continuous Process Improvement', 'Highest
Quality', JSON.stringify(cmmi3))" />
<p:commandButton value="CMMI5" type="button"
onclick="applyData('Process Standardization', 'Medium Quality ',
JSON.stringify(cmmi5))" />
</p:panel>
```

2.  Run the application and navigate to the browser URL
    `http://localhost:8080/jobhub/views/employerslist.xhtml`.

Click on the **CMMI3** and **CMMI5** level buttons to get the company standards. Now you can see the JavaScript parameters assigned to the bean property, as shown in the following screenshot:

Here, we used the JsonConverter component for converting the company standards from the JSON string representation to a bean property.

# Working with advanced dynamic forms and editor components

This section explains the advanced Dynaform component for dynamic form creation and editor components such as CKEditor and codeMirror for a user-friendly interface.

## DynaForm

The JSF or PrimeFaces panelGrid component can be used to create static forms based on the column count, row count, and positions of the elements. However, the panelGrid component is not useful for dynamic form creation at runtime. For example, the dynamic forms will be very helpful if the form is placed in a database or XML file.

The DynaForm component was created to achieve dynamic forms that include labels, input, select components, and many other form components with the help of model creation.

The following are the major features of this component:

- Extended view or grid area
- Open or close state saving
- Auto submit functionality
- Various facets – regular, extended, and button bar
- JavaScript widget functions

The DynaForm component will be created with the help of the parent `dynaForm` tag and the child `dynaFormControl` tag that are used to hold basic form components in the XHTML code .The datamodel created in the server-side Java code can be accessed through the `value` attribute of the `dynaForm` tag.

The following five steps need to be iterated for DynaForm model creation:

1. Create an instance of model.
2. Add a row to the regular grid.
3. Add a label.
4. Add an editable control.
5. Create a relationship between the label and control; this step is optional.

The following code creates a Dynaform component with `dynaFormControl` to hold the form components as its children:

```
<pe:dynaForm id="dynaForm" value="#{dynaFormController.model}"
  var="data">
        <pe:dynaFormControl type="input" for="text">
            <p:inputText id="text" value="#{data.value}"
               required="#{data.required}"/>
        </pe:dynaFormControl>
        <pe:dynaFormControl type="select" for="select"
          styleClass="select">
            <p:selectOneMenu id="select" value="#{data.value}"
               required="#{data.required}">
               <f:selectItems value="#{dynaFormController.
                  languages}"/>
            </p:selectOneMenu>
        </pe:dynaFormControl>
</pe:dynaform>
```

The DynaForm model needs to be created using Java code that is accessible through the `value` attribute of the DynaForm component in the XHTML code; this is shown in the following code:

```
protected void initialize() {
        DynaFormModel model = new DynaFormModel();
    // First row
        DynaFormRow row = model.createRegularRow();
        DynaFormLabel label11 = row.addLabel("Author");
        DynaFormControl control12 = row.addControl(new
          BookProperty("Author", true), "input");
        label11.setForControl(control12);
        DynaFormLabel label13 = row.addLabel("ISBN");
        DynaFormControl control14 = row.addControl(new
          BookProperty("ISBN", true), "input");
        label13.setForControl(control14);
        // second  row
        row = model.createRegularRow();
    DynaFormLabel label21 = row.addLabel("Language");
    DynaFormControl control22 = row.addControl(new
      BookProperty("Language", false), "select");
    label41.setForControl(control42);
    DynaFormLabel label23 = row.addLabel("Description", 1, 2);
    DynaFormControl control24 = row.addControl(new
      BookProperty("Description", false), "textarea", 1, 2);
    label43.setForControl(control24);
        }
```

The preceding model is created by attaching the form components to the `dynaFormControl` instance.

# Advanced forms

You can create advanced forms with the help of autoSubmit, an extended view area, various facets, and the open or close state save features. The autoSubmit feature allows us to submit forms on page load time with the form parameters in the URL. The extended view area feature expands dynamic forms with the help of widget functions.

The advanced DynaForm components also support various types of facets such as the header, footer, and button bar for better customization and manages the open or closed states automatically.

The following XHTML code creates a DynaForm component with advanced extended rows:

```
<pe:dynaForm id="dynaForm" value="#{dynaFormController.model}"
  var="data" autoSubmit="true" buttonBarPosition="both"
  widgetVar="dynaFormWidget">
        <pe:dynaFormControl styleClass="pe-dynaform-label">
            <h:outputText value="#{data}"/>
        </pe:dynaFormControl>
<f:facet name="headerRegular">
        <div><h:outputText value="This is a regular header
            area"/></div>
        </f:facet>
        <f:facet name="footerRegular">
            <div><h:outputText value="This is a regular footer
            area"/></div>
        </f:facet>
        <f:facet name="headerExtended">
            <div><h:outputText value="This is an extended header
            area"/></div>
        </f:facet>
        <f:facet name="footerExtended">
            <div><h:outputText value="This is an extended footer
            area"/></div>
        </f:facet>
        <f:facet name="buttonBar">
```

```
<p:commandButton value="Search" action="#{dynaFormController.
  submitForm}" process="dynaForm" update=":mainForm:dynaFormGroup
  :mainForm:inputValues" oncomplete="handleComplete(xhr, status,
  args)"/>
            <p:commandButton type="reset" value="Reset" style="margin-
              left: 5px;"/>
            <p:commandButton type="button" value="Show / hide advanced
              search" style="margin-left: 5px;"
              onclick="PF('dynaFormWidget').toggleExtended()"/>
        </f:facet>
    </pe:dynaForm>
```

In the preceding DynaForm code, you can toggle the extended row from the button bar.

# Model creation in the server-side Java code

Model creation for the advanced DynaForm component is similar to the basic DynaForm component but with the addition of extended rows in the model; the following is the addition that needs to be made:

```
row = model.createExtendedRow();
row.addControl("Permanant address details description", 2, 1);
        row.addControl(new InventoryProperty("(5,2)", false), "desc",
          4, 1);
```

You can also create a single Dynaform component on the frontend but with multiple models in the server-side code. You can switch the models through command actions.

The following code represents multiple models created in server-side Java code; these models will be toggled in the XHTML code:

```
private DynaFormModel modelOne;
 private DynaFormModel modelTwo;
 private boolean showModelOne = true;

 public DynaFormModel getModel() {
        return (showModelOne ? getModelOne() : getModelTwo());
    }
 public DynaFormModel getModelOne() {
        if (modelOne != null) {
            return modelOne;
        }
        modelOne = new DynaFormModel();
```

```
DynaFormRow row = modelOne.createRegularRow();
DynaFormLabel label11 = row.addLabel("Short Name", 1, 1);
DynaFormLabel label12 = row.addLabel("Street", 2, 1);

row = modelOne.createRegularRow();
DynaFormControl control21 = row.addControl(new
  FormField(true), "name", 1, 1);
DynaFormControl control22 = row.addControl(new
  FormField(false), "address", 2, 1);
label11.setForControl(control21);
}

public DynaFormModel getModelTwo() {
    if (modelTwo != null) {
        return modelTwo;
    }
    modelTwo = new DynaFormModel();
    DynaFormRow row = modelTwo.createRegularRow();

    row.addControl("Audio Volume", "separator", 3, 1);
}
```

Based on the command action selection, any one model will be accessed at a time.

# Container Client ID and access controls with VisitCallbacks

A container client ID named varContainerId is very useful to identify the whole client ID of a component that resides in the dynaFormControl component. The value of varContainerId is used to refer to the client ID prefix of the component within the dynaFormControl component. The most common example of this feature is accessing components within the JavaScript code and updating them with the RequestContext utility.

The following XHTML code creates Dynaform with containerID for the RequestContext operations:

```
<pe:dynaForm id="dynaForm" value="#{dynaFormController.model}"
             var="data" varContainerId="ccId">
    <pe:dynaFormControl for="txt">
            <p:inputText id="txt" value="#{data.value}"/>
<p:commandButton icon="ui-icon-search" process="@this txt"
  title="Please choose an item">
```

```
        <f:setPropertyActionListener value="#{ccId}"
          target="#{dynaFormController.containerClientId}"/>
  </p:commandButton>
        </pe:dynaFormControl>
  </pe:dynaForm>
```

The following server-side code represents the component update using the `varContainerID` defined in the XHTML code:

```
private String containerClientId;
private FormField selectedField;
private String selectedItem;
public void updateSelection() {
        FacesContext fc = FacesContext.getCurrentInstance();
        RequestContext rc = RequestContext.getCurrentInstance();
        // update the corresponding input field in UI
        rc.update(containerClientId + UINamingContainer.
getSeparatorChar(fc) + "text");
    }
```

In the preceding code, `RequestContext` updated the component with the help of the container client ID.

# VisitCallbacks

The VisitCallbacks feature allows you to visit all the controls inside Dynaform and executes certain tasks on them. First, you have to create an executable task implementation for `VisitTaskExecutor` and then assign this implementation task to the `ExecutableVisitCallback` interface.

The best example for this feature is to visit all the specified components in the Dynaform control and execute some tasks on them. The task implementation class `ClearInputsExecutor` of the `VisitTaskExecutor` interface is used to clear the input fields and assigns the task instance to the visit callback interface named `ExecutableVisitCallback`.

We have to provide the row and column indices for each component through the condition implementation defined on the server side.

The following XHTML code represents the Dynaform component `visitCallbacks` and `clearInputExecutor`:

```
<pe:dynaForm id="dynaForm" value="#{dynaFormController.model}"
  var="condition">
<pe:dynaFormControl type="column">
```

```
            <p:selectOneMenu id="tableColumn" value="#{condition.
              tableColumn}">
                <f:selectItem itemValue="" itemLabel=""/>
                <f:selectItem itemValue="model" itemLabel="model"/>
                <f:selectItem itemValue="manufacturer"
                   itemLabel="manufacturer"/>
                <f:selectItem itemValue="year" itemLabel="year"/>
                <f:attribute name="rcIndex" value="#{condition.index}"/>
            </p:selectOneMenu>
        </pe:dynaFormControl>
        <pe:dynaFormControl type="offset">
            <p:spinner id="inputOffset" value="#{condition.inputOffset}"
              min="0" max="99">
                <pe:keyFilter mask="num"/>
                <f:attribute name="rcIndex" value="#{condition.index}"/>
            </p:spinner>
        </pe:dynaFormControl>
    <pe:dynaFormControl type="operator">
     <p:selectOneMenu id="valueOperator" value="#{condition.
       valueOperator}">
                <f:selectItem itemValue="eq" itemLabel="equal"/>
                <f:selectItem itemValue="not" itemLabel="not equal"/>
                <f:attribute name="rcIndex" value="#{condition.index}"/>
    </pe:dynaFormControl>
    <pe:dynaFormControl type="value">
            <p:inputText id="inputValue" value="#{condition.inputValue}">
                <f:attribute name="rcIndex" value="#{condition.index}"/>
            </p:inputText>
        </pe:dynaFormControl>
    <pe:dynaFormControl type="clear" styleClass="clearLink">
            <p:commandLink value="Clear inputs" process="@this"
              action="#{dynaFormController.clearInputs(condition.index)}"
              global="false"/>
        </pe:dynaFormControl>
    </pe:dynaForm>
```

The model can be created on the server side through multiple conditions. For this, we first have to define the conditions for each component and then clear inputs through the `ClearInputVisitTaskExecutor` implementation and `ExecutableVisitCallback` interface.

```
protected void initialize() {
        model = new DynaFormModel();
        conditions = new ArrayList<Condition>();
```

```
Condition condition = new Condition("model", 2, "eq",
    "mercedes", 0);
conditions.add(condition);
DynaFormRow row = model.createRegularRow();
row.addControl(condition, "column");
row.addControl(condition, "offset");
row.addControl(condition, "operator");
row.addControl(condition, "value");
row.addControl(condition, "clear");
}
```

The following method is used to clear all the inputs by visiting the components one by one:

```
public void clearInputs(int index) {
    FacesContext fc = FacesContext.getCurrentInstance();
    DynaForm dynaForm = (DynaForm) fc.getViewRoot().findComponent(
        ":mainForm:dynaForm");
    // Ids of components to be visited
    String[] ids = new String[] {"tableColumn", "inputValue",
        "inputOffset", "valueOperator"};
    VisitTaskExecutor visitTaskExecutor = new
        ClearInputsExecutor(fc.getELContext(), RequestContext.
        getCurrentInstance(), ids, index);
    // clear inputs in the visit callback
    ExecutableVisitCallback visitCallback = new ExecutableVisitCal
        lback(visitTaskExecutor);
    dynaForm.visitTree(VisitContext.createVisitContext(fc, null,
        VISIT_HINTS), visitCallback);
}
```

In the preceding code, all the form components are visited first and the input values will be cleared through command actions.

# JobHub in action

Let us use the advanced features of Dynaform, such as the various facets and extended view grid area in our JobHub application; this is shown in a step-by-step manner:

1. Create the following XHTML code that contains an advanced Dynaform component with extended rows, which binds it to datamodel from the server-side code:

```
<pe:dynaForm id="dynaForm" value="#{employeeRegistration.model}"
    var="data" autoSubmit="true" buttonBarPosition="bottom"
    widgetVar="dynaFormWidget">
        <pe:dynaFormControl styleClass="pe-dynaform-label">
```

```
    <h:outputText value="#{data}" />
    </pe:dynaFormControl>
    <pe:dynaFormControl type="input" for="input">
    <p:inputText id="input" value="#{data.value}"
      required="#{data.required}" />
    </pe:dynaFormControl>
    <pe:dynaFormControl type="select1" for="country"
      styleClass="select">
    <p:selectOneMenu id="country" value="#{data.value}"
      required="#{data.required}">
<f:selectItems value="#{employeeRegistration.countries}" />
    </p:selectOneMenu>
    </pe:dynaFormControl>
    <pe:dynaFormControl type="select2" for="city"
      styleClass="select">
    <p:selectOneMenu id="city" value="#{data.value}"
      required="#{data.required}">
<f:selectItems value="#{employeeRegistration.cities}" />
    </p:selectOneMenu>
    </pe:dynaFormControl>
    <pe:dynaFormControl type="select3" for="country"
      styleClass="select">
    <p:selectOneMenu id="country1" value="#{data.value}"
      widgetVar="$country1" required="#{data.required}">
<f:selectItems value="#{employeeRegistration.countries}" />
    </p:selectOneMenu>
    </pe:dynaFormControl>
    <pe:dynaFormControl type="select4" for="city"
      styleClass="select" widgetVar="$city1">
    <p:selectOneMenu id="city1" value="#{data.value}"
      required="#{data.required}">
<f:selectItems value="#{employeeRegistration.cities}" />
    </p:selectOneMenu>
    </pe:dynaFormControl>
    <pe:dynaFormControl type="desc" for="desc">
    <p:inputTextarea id="desc" value="#{data.value}"
      required="#{data.required}" autoResize="false" />
    </pe:dynaFormControl>
    <f:facet name="headerRegular">
<div>
<h:outputText value="Current Address details" />
</div>
    </f:facet>
    <f:facet name="headerExtended">
<div>
```

```
        <h:outputText value="Permanent Address details" />
    </div>
        </f:facet>
        <f:facet name="buttonBar">
        <p:commandButton type="button" value="Show/hide Permanent
address details" style="margin-left: 5px;"
        onclick="PF('dynaFormWidget').toggleExtended();" />
        </f:facet>
</pe:dynaForm>
```

2. Create the following JSF-managed bean code that consists of the advanced DynaForm data model:

```
@PostConstruct
public void init() {
  model = new DynaFormModel();
            DynaFormRow row = model.createRegularRow();
  DynaFormLabel label11 = row.addLabel("Address", 1, 1);
  DynaFormControl control12 = row.addControl(new AddressProperty(
        "Address", false), "input", 2, 1);
            label11.setForControl(control12);
  DynaFormControl control13 = row.addControl(new AddressProperty(
        "Address", false), "input", 1, 1);
  row = model.createRegularRow();
  DynaFormLabel label21 = row.addLabel("Country", 1, 1);
  DynaFormControl control22 = row.addControl(new AddressProperty(
        "Country", true), "select1", 1, 1);
  label21.setForControl(control22);
  DynaFormLabel label23 = row.addLabel("City", 1, 1);
  DynaFormControl control24 = row.addControl(new
AddressProperty("City",
        "Select", true), "select2", 1, 1);
  label23.setForControl(control24);
  row = model.createRegularRow();
  DynaFormLabel label31 = row.addLabel(
  "Email (this field requires any not empty input)", 3, 1);
DynaFormControl control32 = row.addControl(new
AddressProperty("Email",true), "input", 1, 1);
  label31.setForControl(control32);
  row = model.createRegularRow();
  DynaFormLabel label41 = row.addLabel("Phone", 1, 1);
  DynaFormControl control42 = row.addControl(new AddressProperty(
        "Extension", true), "input", 1, 1);
  label41.setForControl(control42);
DynaFormControl control43 = row.addControl(new
AddressProperty("Phone",true), "input", 2, 1);
  row = model.createRegularRow();
  DynaFormLabel label51 = row.addLabel("Mobile", 1, 1);
```

```
DynaFormControl control52 = row.addControl(new AddressProperty(
    "Mobile", true), "input", 1, 1);
label51.setForControl(control52);
DynaFormLabel label53 = row.addLabel("Description", 1, 2);
DynaFormControl control54 = row.addControl(new AddressProperty(
    "Moreinfo", false), "desc", 1, 1);
label53.setForControl(control54);
row = model.createRegularRow();
DynaFormLabel label61 = row.addLabel("Zip code", 1, 1);
DynaFormControl control62 = row.addControl(new
AddressProperty("Zip",true), "input", 1, 1);
label61.setForControl(control62);
row = model.createExtendedRow();
row.addControl("Address", 1, 1);
row.addControl(new AddressProperty("Address", false), "input",
2, 1);
row.addControl(new AddressProperty("Address", false), "input",
1, 1);
row = model.createExtendedRow();
row.addControl("Country", 1, 1);
row.addControl(new AddressProperty("Country", false), "select3",
1, 1);
row.addControl("City", 1, 1);
row.addControl(new AddressProperty("City", false), "select4", 1,
1);
}
```

3. Run the application and navigate to the following browser URL:
   `http://localhost:8080/jobhub/views/employeeRegistration.xhtml`

Now you are able to see the dynamic form that is generated for the **Address** tab field displayed in the registration form, as shown in the following screenshot:

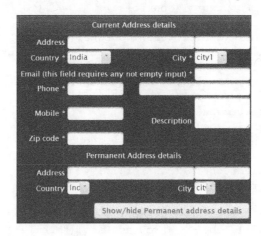

Now you have created the JobSeeker address details with advanced DynaForm features.

# CKEditor

The CKEditor is a WYSIWYG text editor that is to be used for the web pages that bring the desktop editing application features from Microsoft Word and OpenOffice to web applications. The text being edited in this editor makes the results similar to what you can see after the web page is published. The CKEditor component is available as a separate JAR file from the Extensions library; this library or dependency needs to be included on demand. Please refer to *Chapter 1, Introducing PrimeFaces Extensions*, for more details.

The CKEditor component provides more custom controls with the custom toolbar template and skinning in user interfaces using the `theme` and `interfaceColor` properties as compared to the PrimeFaces editor component.

The editor component is, by default, displayed with all the controls to make the content customizable. You can supply a few more customizations through `interfaceColor` to change the interface dynamically and `checkDirtyInterval` for repeated time interval checks after the content has been changed. To make asynchronous communication calls on the server-side code, many Ajax events are supported by this component.

The following XHTML code creates a CKEditor component with custom interface colors:

```
<pe:ckEditor id="editor" value="#{ckeditorController.content}" interfa
  ceColor="#{ckeditorController.color}" checkDirtyInterval="0">
    <p:ajax event="save" listener="#{ckeditorController.saveListener}"
      update="growl"/>
</pe:ckEditor>
```

You can write any number of instances on the same page. There are two ways in which we can customize the CKEditor toolbar component:

1. **Toolbar defined with default custom controls**: You can customize the editor toolbar by declaring the control names in the form of a string name or an array of strings.

2. **CustomConfig JavaScript file for user-defined controls**: You can also customize the toolbar by defining the custom config JavaScript file through the `customConfig` attribute and register the control configuration names on the `toolbar` attribute.

The following XHTML code creates the CKEditor toolbar with custom controls:

```
<pe:ckEditor id="editor" value="#{ckeditorController.content}" toolbar
   ="[['Cut','Copy','Paste','PasteText','PasteFromWord']]">
  <p:ajax event="save" listener="#{ckeditorController.saveListener}"
    update="growl"/>
</pe:ckEditor>
```

# JobHub in action

Let us modify the JobHub application footer information such as about us, communication, privacy, disclaimer, and privacy details with the help of the Extensions CKEditor component by logging in as the admin; the following are the steps to do so:

1.  Create XHTML code that contains the CKEditor component to modify the "about us" footer configuration details. You can customize the toolbar controls and interface colors through the toolbar and interfaceColor attributes respectively; this is shown in the following code:

```
<p:accordionPanel activeIndex="-1">
    <p:tab title="AboutUS">
    <h:panelGrid id="aboutusgrid" columns="2" cellpadding="10">
    <p:graphicImage value="/resources/images/aboutus.png" />
    <h:outputText value="#{adminController.aboutus}" />
    </h:panelGrid>
  <p:commandButton value="Edit" actionListener="#{adminController.
    aboutusEdit}"
  update="editor1panel"></p:commandButton>
  <p:outputPanel id="editor1panel">
  <pe:ckEditor id="editor1" value="#{adminController.aboutus}"
    toolbar="[['Cut','Copy','Paste','PasteText','PasteFromWo
    rd','-', 'SpellChecker']]" interfaceColor="\##{adminControll
    er.color1}"  rendered="#{adminController.aboutusFlag}"
    width="500" />
  <p:outputPanel rendered="#{adminController.aboutusFlag}">
  <p:colorPicker id="popupCP1" value="#{adminController.color1}">
  </p:colorPicker>
  <p:commandButton value="Submit color" update="editor1" />
  </p:outputPanel>
```

```
<p:commandButton value="Save" actionListener="#{adminController.
  aboutusSave}" update="editor1panel,aboutusgrid"
  rendered="#{adminController.aboutusFlag}"></p:commandButton>
</p:outputPanel>
  </p:tab>
</p:accordionPanel>
```

2. Create a JSF-managed bean that holds the "about us" section under the footer configuration details:

```
@ManagedBean
@ApplicationScoped
public class AdminController implements Serializable {
  private static final long serialVersionUID = 1L;
  private String aboutus;
  private String communication;
  private String privacy;
  private String disclaimer;
  private String help;
  private String color="1234FF";
  @PostConstruct
  public void init() {
  aboutus = "Some content goes here";
  }
  public void aboutusEdit() {
    aboutusFlag = true;
  }
  public void aboutusSave() {
    aboutus = aboutus.replaceAll("\\<.*?>","");
    aboutusFlag = false;
  }
//getters and setters
}
```

3. Run the application and navigate to the admin page with the browser URL http://localhost:8080/jobhub/views/admin.xhtml using the admin role.

Now you can see the **About Us** tab under the footer configuration. Clicking on the **Edit** button renders the editor component as shown in the following screenshot:

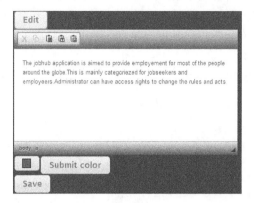

Change the **About Us** information and click on the **Save** button. Now you will have the updated content for the about us section throughout the JobHub application; this is shown in the following screenshot:

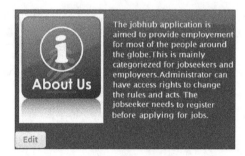

Thus CKEditor updated the footer configuration details throughout the application.

# CodeMirror

CodeMirror is a JavaScript library that creates a pleasant user interface for the coding part in your web pages. The coding section includes HTML markup and computer programs. Defining the mode property allows coloring the content, font indentation, and a few CSS styles.

The following CSS styles are available to the code mirror component:

- `codemirror/mode/spec.css`
- `codemirror/mode/tiddlywiki.css`
- `codemirror/mode/tiki.css`

You can include the preceding CSS styles through the JSF outputStyleSheet declaration on the top of your page.

The CodeMirror component is available as a separate JAR file from the Extensions library and this library or dependency needs to be included on demand. Please refer to *Chapter 1*, *Introducing PrimeFaces Extensions*, for more details.

You can update the editor content through Ajax calls via the mode that refers to different MIME types.

The following XHTML code creates CodeMirror for different modes that refer the various MIME types:

```
<pe:codeMirror id="codeMirror" mode="#{codeMirrorController.mode}"
    theme="eclipse" value="#{codeMirrorController.content}"
    lineNumbers="true"/>
<p:commandButton actionListener="#{codeMirrorController.changeMode}"
  update="codeMirror"  value="Change mode with AJAX"/>
//Change the MIME type from javascript to css type
public void changeMode() {
        if (mode.equals("css")) {
            mode = "javascript";
        } else {
            mode = "css";
        }
    }
```

CodeMirror allows the code completion of your script via completeMethod using the key combination (*Ctrl* + Space bar). The code completion is activated through the extraKeys attributes.

The following XHTML code creates CodeMirror for the code completion functionality:

```
<pe:codeMirror id="codeMirror"
    mode="#{codeMirrorController.mode}"
    widgetVar="myCodeMirror"
    theme="eclipse" value="#{codeMirrorController.content}"
    lineNumbers="true"
    completeMethod="#{codeMirrorController.complete}"
    extraKeys="{ 'Ctrl-Space': function(cm) { PF('myCodeMirror').
    complete(); }}" />
```

In the preceding code example, the mode property refers to the type of script or language used and the color of the text changed based on the mode name.

The following code changes the mode name based on the user command action:

```
public void changeMode() {
        if (mode.equals("css")) {
            mode = "javascript";
        } else {
            mode = "css";
        }
}
```

CodeMirror has built-in support for JavaScript code completion through the JavaScript hint that exists in the code mirror script file.

The following XHTML code represents the CodeMirror component with JavaScript code completion support:

```
<pe:codeMirror id="codeMirror" mode="#{codeMirrorController.
    mode}"  theme="eclipse" value="#{codeMirrorController.content}"
    lineNumbers="true"
    extraKeys="{ 'Ctrl-Space': function(cm) {CodeMirror.
    simpleHint(cm,CodeMirror.javascriptHint);}}" />
```

Now CodeMirror will support the code completion feature through the *Ctrl* + Space bar key combination.

# Summary

In this chapter, you have been introduced to enhanced form input components such as InputNumber, KeyFilter, TriState checkboxes, tooltip, remoteCommand, and their major features. You also learned about the advanced Dynaform and editor components, such as CKEditor and CodeMirror, for user-friendly interfaces.

In the next chapter, we will take a detailed look at the Layout components, Scroll context components such as WayPoint, components for layout design, blocking the user interface in web pages, and looking at their role in application development.

# 3
# Layout and Screen Blocking Components

The PrimeFaces Extensions team has introduced a controlled and enhanced **Layout** component, a scroll context component named **Waypoint**, and screen blocking components such as **BlockUI** and **Spotlight** to optimize web page design. The layout component is aimed at creating the templating mechanism in a JSF-based application, the Waypoint component is used for executing custom logic when scrolled to a particular component, and screen blocking components such as BlockUI and Spotlight are used to block a certain part of the web page.

In this chapter, we will cover the following topics:

- Creating pages based on the layout component and understanding their features
- Waypoint as a scroll context component and its features
- BlockUI and Spotlight screen blocking components and their features

## Creating pages based on the layout component and understanding their features

Layout components are used to design web page structure and categorize the various functionalities in different areas of the page. This layout component provides features such as state management, custom content between layouts, and more optimized layout options. It also provides objects such as iframe inside layout panes, which are not available in the PrimeFaces Core component. Layout component creates a border layout for the web page, which includes an auto-sizing center pane. It can also be surrounded by four closable and resizable border panes with respect to the four directions (north, south, east, and west) of the web page.

You can create complex layouts by nesting the layout inside another layout component. Both server-side and client-side state managements are available to this component.

Each layout pane (except the center layout pane) can be closed, opened, and resized automatically or specific to certain limits. The layout contains a header at the top of each pane. You can also place the custom content between the layout panes.

The layout component is created based on jQuery layout plugins, which include all possible layout options. It was backed by the model that binds all the options together and the layout options built by the LayoutOptions class. The model is defined as layout options in the backing bean of layout components.

The layout component supports the following list of events:

- Open
- Close
- Resize

# State management

The state property or attribute defines the server-side state management. This can be represented in a JSON string that contains all dimensions, open or close state information of existing layout panes, and is bound to a backing bean property.

Client state management is enabled by setting stateCookie="true". By default, stateCookie is set to false. When you configure a layout to client-side state management (stateCookie=true), the layout state will be stored in a cookie on Windows, unloaded and restored during the layout build-up by postback calls.

# Layout options

The layout component describes the options either through the LayoutOptions model or direct attributes of the pe:layout component. To use fully controlled LayoutOptions or a limited set of options via attributes is totally dependent on the functional requirement.

# Layout categories

Basically, layout supports two types of layout structures. The following two types of layout categories are used:

- **Full page layout**: This defines layout for an entire page
- **Element layout**: This defines layout for a specific region in the web page

# Layout features

Layout component features are categorized into the following five sections:

- The element layout and server-side management
- The full-page layout and client-side management
- Layout options as tag attributes
- Custom content between layout panes
- Layout with iframe

# The element layout and server-side management

The layout is defined for a specific part of the web page by setting `fullPage="false"`.

The following code represents the element layout with server-side state management:

```
<pe:layout fullPage="false" style="width:450px; height:220px;"
    options="#{layoutController.layoutOptions}"
        state="#{layoutController.state}">
        <pe:layoutPane position="west">
            Left
        </pe:layoutPane>
        <pe:layoutPane position="center">
            Center
        </pe:layoutPane>
</pe:layout>
```

The following code represents layout options to provide custom options in the backing bean:

```
private LayoutOptions layoutOptions;

@PostConstruct
protected void initialize() {
 layoutOptions = new LayoutOptions();
 //Options for all panes
 LayoutOptions panes = new LayoutOptions();
 panes.addOption("slidable", false);
 panes.addOption("resizeWhileDragging", true);
 layoutOptions.setPanesOptions(panes);

 //Set options for west pane
 LayoutOptions left = new LayoutOptions();
 left.addOption("size", 150);
```

```
left.addOption("minSize", 40);
left.addOption("maxSize", 300);
layoutOptions.setWestOptions(left);

//set options for center pane
layoutOptionsTwo = new LayoutOptions();

    // options for all panes
LayoutOptions center= new LayoutOptions();
center.addOption("size", 200);
center.addOption("minSize", 50);
center.addOption("maxSize", 250);
layoutOptions.setWestOptions(center);
}
```

# The full-page layout and client-side management

The layout defined for entire web page results in a border layout is called a full-page layout. By default, layout is a full-page layout; you can change to the element layout by setting `fullPage` to `false`.

Layout supports a few of the client-side widget methods such as `sizePane()`, `sizeContent()`, `open()`, `close()`, and `toggle()` for layout pane manipulation. All these methods expect layout position as a parameter and nested pane position names are concatenated by the underscore ("_") sign.

 Center panes cannot be manipulated. Any client-side methods on a center pane (as a center pane position parameter) results in invalid calls. For example, `open("center")` results in an invalid call.

The following code represents the full-page layout with client state management:

```
<pe:layout id="fullPage"
    options="#{layoutController.layoutOptions}"
            stateCookie="true" widgetVar="fpLayoutWidget">

        <pe:layoutPane position="north">
            North
        </pe:layoutPane>
        <pe:layoutPane position="center">
            Center
        </pe:layoutPane>
```

```
<pe:layoutPane position="west">
    West
</pe:layoutPane>
<pe:layoutPane position="east">
    <pe:layoutPane position="north">
        West-North
    </pe:layoutPane>
    <pe:layoutPane position="center">
        West-Center
    </pe:layoutPane>
    <pe:layoutPane position="south">
        West-South
    </pe:layoutPane>
</pe:layoutPane>
<pe:layoutPane position="south">
    South
</pe:layoutPane>
</pe:layout>
```

You can apply the following client-side functions inside any one of the layout panes in order to see their features:

```
<h:panelGrid columns="6" style="margin-left:80px;">
<p:commandButton value="Toggle South" type="button"
  onclick="PF('fpLayoutWidget').close('south')"/>
<p:commandButton value="Toggle West-North" type="button"
  onclick="PF('fpLayoutWidget').open('south')"/>
<p:commandButton value="Close Center-North" type="button"
  onclick="PF('fpLayoutWidget').toggle('east_south')"/>
<p:commandButton value="Size East Pane" type="button"
  onclick="PF('fpLayoutWidget').sizePane('west', 350)"/>
</h:panelGrid>
```

Here we created a simple full-page layout with client-side widget functions for layout pane manipulations.

# Layout options as tag attributes

You can also create layout options by defining the attributes to layout and LayoutPane components. For example, you can customize the default tooltips of open, close, and resized operations via attributes.

 LayoutPane has a limited set of options via attributes in comparison to the generic approach provided by the LayoutOptions model in the managed bean.

The following layout code represents layout options such as open and closed tooltips for layout with `size`, `minHeight`, and `closable` for the LayoutPane components via attributes:

```
<pe:layout resizerTip="Resize Me" togglerTipClosed="Open Me"
    togglerTipOpen="Close Me">
        <pe:layoutPane position="north" size="60" >
        <f:facet name="header">
                    <h:outputText value="North"/>
            </f:facet>
        </pe:layoutPane>
        <pe:layoutPane position="center">
            <pe:layoutPane position="north" size="40%"
                minHeight="60">
                Center-North
            </pe:layoutPane>
            <pe:layoutPane position="center" >
                Center-center
            </pe:layoutPane>
        <pe:layoutPane position="south" size="40%"
            initClosed="true">
                Center-South
            </pe:layoutPane>
        </pe:layoutPane>
        <pe:layoutPane position="west" size="300"
            resizeWhileDragging="true">
            West
        </pe:layoutPane>
        <pe:layoutPane position="east" size="300" >
            East
        </pe:layoutPane>
        <pe:layoutPane position="south" size="60"
            closable="false">
            South
        </pe:layoutPane>
    </pe:layout>
```

# Custom content between layout panes

You can also add custom content between the layout panes in three different ways, as follows:

- Add a nested layout panel inside the `div` element with the class "ui-layout-pane".

- Add the `containerSelector` option for the child options of the `LayoutOptions` class. The value of `containerSelector` refers to the `wrapper-div` element and acts as a container for nested layout pane.

- Use the header facet of LayoutPane to stick the content when scrolling the page.

Use the following XHTML code to add custom content between layout panes using the nested layout panel inside the `div` element or the header facets of layout pane:

```
<pe:layout resizerTip="Resize Me" togglerTipClosed="Open Me"
    togglerTipOpen="Close Me">
        <pe:layoutPane position="north" size="60" >
            <f:facet name="header">
                    <h:outputText value="North"/>
                </f:facet>
        </pe:layoutPane>
        <pe:layoutPane position="center">
            <div class="ui-layout-content">
        <pe:layoutPane position="north" size="40%" minHeight="60">
                Center-North
            </pe:layoutPane>
            <pe:layoutPane position="center" >
                Center-center
            </pe:layoutPane>

    </div>
        </pe:layoutPane>
        <pe:layoutPane position="west" size="300"
            resizeWhileDragging="true">
            West
        </pe:layoutPane>
        <pe:layoutPane position="east" size="300" >
            East
        </pe:layoutPane>
        <pe:layoutPane position="south" size="60"
            closable="false">
            South
        </pe:layoutPane>
    </pe:layout>
```

# IFrame objects in layout panes

You can use an iframe as a layout pane without worrying about any resizing issues by just setting `maskContents="true"`. To use iframe as a layout pane, you just need to place the iframe as the direct child of layout pane.

> If you use an iframe as layout pane, then it is recommended to add `maskContents=true` to overcome resizing issues. If you use objects such as applets, Google Maps, and so on as layout panes, then it is recommended to add `maskObject=true`. Both iframe and objects such as applets and Google Maps placed inside LayoutPane require `maskPanesEarly` set to `true` on layout component.

The following XHTML code is used to represent an iframe that navigates to PrimeFaces Extensions to showcase a site that acts as LayoutPane:

```
<pe:layout maskPanesEarly="true">
    <pe:layoutPane position="north" size="100">
            North
    </pe:layoutPane>
    <pe:layoutPane position="center" maskContents="true">
    <iframe id="iframeCenter"
        src="http://www.primefaces.org/showcase-
        ext/views/home.jsf" width="100%" height="100%"
        frameborder="0">
    </iframe>
    </pe:layoutPane>
    <pe:layoutPane position="south" size="100"
            maxSize="200" minSize="50">
            south
    </pe:layoutPane>
</pe:layout>
```

In the previous code section, an `iframe` object is placed inside the center LayoutPane.

# JobHub in action

Let us introduce layout features such as the element layout, nested layouts, and state management in the EmployersList and JobsList screens.

Let us start with the layout features of the **EmployersList** screen, as follows:

1. Create an XHTML code that provides a basic layout mechanism with the element layout, nested layouts, and server-side state management features in the EmployersList screen.

```
<pe:layout resizerTip="Resize Me"
    togglerTipClosed="Open Me"
    fullPage="false"
    state="#{employerDetailsController.state}"
    style="width:100%; height:650px;"
    togglerTipOpen="Close Me">
    <pe:layoutPane position="east" size="300">
        <f:facet name="header">
            Latest Updates
        </f:facet>
        // recent updates in table format goes here
    </pe:layoutPane>
    <pe:layoutPane position="center" update="">
        <h:form id="employerForm">
        //employer details and reports goes here
    </h:form>
    </pe:layoutPane>
    <pe:layoutPane position="west" size="400">
        <f:facet name="header">
            New Employer Registration
        </f:facet>
    <pe:layoutPane position="north">
        <h:form id="registration">
        //employer registration goes here
        </h:form>
    </pe:layoutPane>
    <pe:layoutPane position="center">
        <h:form id="standards">
        // company standards goes here
        </h:form>
    </pe:layoutPane>
    </pe:layoutPane>
</pe:layout>
```

2. Run the application and navigate to the employer's EmployersList page with the URL `http://localhost:8080/jobhub/views/employerslist.xhtml` using the employer's role.

Now you are able to see the element layout with the nested layouts feature, as follows:

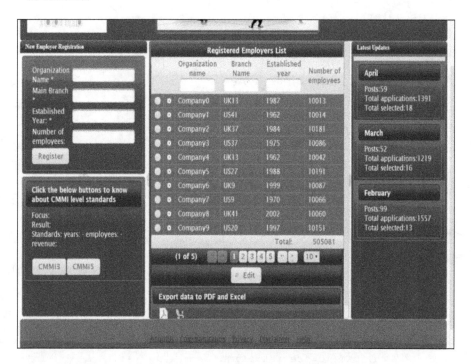

You can close, open, resize, and scroll (if it exists) the layout based on interest. Here, the element layout covers employer registration and standards in the west position, a registered employers list in the center, and the latest updates in the east position.

We will next use layout features such as the element layout and client-side state management in the JobsList screen, as follows:

1. Create an XHTML code that contains layout features such as the element layout and client-state management in the JobsList screen.

```xml
<pe:layout resizerTip="Resize Me"
togglerTipClosed="Open Me"
    fullPage="false" stateCookie="true" style="width:100%;
    height:650px;"
    togglerTipOpen="Close Me">
    <pe:layoutPane position="east" size="300">
        <f:facet name="header">
                Latest Updates
        </f:facet>
        //Latest updates in table format goes here
    </pe:layoutPane>
    <pe:layoutPane position="center">
        <h:form id="masterDetailform">
        // List of posts,jobcategories,skills details using
        masterDetail
        // component goes here
        </h:form>
    </pe:layoutPane>
    <pe:layoutPane position="west" size="200">
    <pe:layoutPane position="north" size="150">
        <f:facet name="header">
            <h:outputText value="Search criteria for Job
                Posts" />
        </f:facet>
            //Job search criteria goes here
        </pe:layoutPane>
        <pe:layoutPane position="center" size="200">
            <f:facet name="header">
            <h:outputText value="Companies List" />
        </f:facet>
        <h:form id="companiesForm">
          //List of companies navigation link goes here
        </h:form>
        </pe:layoutPane>
        </pe:layoutPane>
    </pe:layout>
```

2. Run the application and navigate to the JobSeeker's **JobsList** page with the URL `http://localhost:8080/jobhub/views/jobsList.xhtml` using the employer's role.

Now you are able to see the element layout with the nested layouts feature and client-side state management, as follows:

Here, the element layout covers the search criteria, a list of all posts, and the latest updates sections in the west, center, and east positions, respectively.

To condense the coding section of the layout design, we just provided the basic template without content. For the complete example code, check `https://github.com/sudheerj/Learning-Primefaces-Extension-Development/tree/master/jobhub`.

# Waypoint as a scroll context component and its features

Waypoint creates modern UI design trends such as a one-page site depending upon scroll position on a page and performs execution of a custom logic when you scroll to a specified element. This component is mostly used for lazy-loading data as a user scrolls the page. It supports both horizontal and vertical scrolling.

The Waypoint component supports only the **reached** event, which is used either by JavaScript or Ajax behavior components. When the scroll goes past the element, the callback function is called to access the scrolling direction ("down", "up", "left", and "right") and the current Waypoint object.

Waypoint supports the following useful client-side widget methods to work with modern UI designs:

- enable()
- disable()

The Waypoint component supports the following list of features or use cases:

- Infinite scrolling
- Sticky elements
- Dial controls
- Scroll analytics

# Infinite scrolling

Infinite scrolling works with the optional remoteCommand component and offset function. The offset defines Waypoint if the bottom of the element is in view and is recalculated based on window size.

Infinite scrolling is useful when you are dealing with big data sets; images loading on demand are the most common use case.

The following XHTML creates the infinite scrolling functionality of the Waypoint component with the animation look and feel of images loading:

```
<img src="data:image/gif;base64,R01GOD1hAQABAAD/ACwAAAAAQABAAACADs="
    data-src="http://farm2.static.flickr.
    com/1275/644620280_25f2c0ca61_m.jpg" width="240" height="180"/>
<img src="data:image/gif;base64,R01GOD1hAQABAAD/
    ACwAAAAAQABAAACADs="data-src="http://farm4.static.flickr.com/3133/
    3145677692_79763f61a5_m.jpg" width="240" height="180"/>

<pe:waypoint id="waypoint" for="@(img[data-src])" offset="'100%'">
    <pe:javascript event="reached"
        execute="handleWaypoint(ext);"/>
</pe:waypoint>
```

The following JavaScript function is called when the Waypoint `reached` event is fired:

```
<h:outputScript id="waypointScript" target="body">
/* <![CDATA[ */
    function handleWaypoint(ext) {
        img.css('opacity', 0);
        img.attr('src', img.attr('data-src'));
        img.load(function(){
            img.animate({ opacity: 1 }, 500);
            img.removeAttr('data-src');
            img.waypoint('destroy');
        });
    }
/* ]]> */
</h:outputScript>
```

The preceding JavaScript function adds various animation features to the image when scroll reaches the offset.

# Sticky elements

**Sticky menu bar** and **back to top** links are well-known modern UI designs built with the help of plain JavaScript. You can use these extensions of Waypoint to easily work with this use case.

When you scroll down the page, you will find that the menu bar gets stuck and a back to top link appears in the bottom right. When you scroll up the page, the menu bar gets unstuck and the back to top link disappears.

The following XHTML code is used to work with the sticky elements feature of Waypoint:

```
<h:panelGroup id="wrapper" layout="block">
    <h:panelGroup id="main-nav-holder" layout="block">
        <p:menubar id="menubar">
            <p:menuitem value="File" url="#" icon="ui-icon-
                document"/>
            <p:menuitem value="New" url="#" icon="ui-icon-
                contact"/>
            <p:menuitem value="Edit" url="#" icon="ui-icon-
                pencil"/>
            <p:menuitem value="Help" url="#" icon="ui-icon-help"/>
        </p:menubar>
    </h:panelGroup>
```

```
  <h:panelGroup id="container" layout="block">
  Content goes here..
  </h:panelGroup>
   <p:commandButton id="topLink" type="button" value="TOP"
       icon="ui-icon-triangle-1-n" styleClass="top hidden"
       title="Back to top" onclick="$('html, body').animate

     ({scrollTop: 0}, 'fast');"/>
</h:panelGroup>
<pe:waypoint id="waypoint1" for="wrapper" offset="'-100%'">
    <pe:javascript event="reached"
        execute="$('#topLink').toggleClass('hidden', ext.direction
        === 'up');"/>
</pe:waypoint>
<pe:waypoint id="waypoint2" for="main-nav-holder">
    <pe:javascript event="reached"
        execute="$(ext.waypoint).toggleClass('sticky',
        ext.direction === 'down');"/>
</pe:waypoint>The following style classes are applied during the whole
    functionality of sticky WayPoint component.
<h:outputStylesheet id="waypointCSS">
    #wrapper {
    width: 560px;
    margin: 0 auto;
      }
    #menubar {
        width: 560px;
      }
    .sticky #menubar {
        position: fixed;
        top: 0;
      }
    #container {
        margin-bottom: 20px;
      }
    .top {
        position: fixed;
        right: 20px;
        bottom: 20px;
        font-size: 14px;
        box-shadow: 0 0 15px 1px #808080;
      }
    .top.hidden {
        display: none;
      }
</h:outputStylesheet>
```

When you scroll the mouse and reach a certain distance from the top, the back to top link will be visible; clicking on the button scrolls the page to the top of the screen.

# Dial controls

You can create the dial controls functionality by the use of Waypoint within scrollable non-window elements with the help of the `forContext` attribute along with the pe:javascript component.

The following XHTML code represents dial controls functionality by controlling the font size of text:

```
<h:panelGroup id="wrapper" layout="block">
    <div data-property="font-size" class="dial first">
    <ul>
            <li data-value="8px">8px</li>
            <li data-value="10px">10px</li>
            <li data-value="12px">12px</li>
            <li data-value="14px">14px</li>
    </ul>
    </div>
</h:panelGroup>

<pe:waypoint id="waypoint" for="@(.dial li)" forContext="@(.dial
    ul)" offset="25">
    <pe:javascript event="reached" execute="handleWaypoint(ext);"/>
</pe:waypoint>
```

The following script changes the CSS styles of defined content using the ClientBehaviours `execute` attribute and should be attached to the Waypoint component:

```
<h:outputScript id="waypointScript" target="body">
/* <![CDATA[ */
    function handleWaypoint(ext) {
        var $active = $(ext.waypoint);

        if (ext.direction === "up") {
            $active = $active.prev();
        }

        if (!$active.length) $active.end();

        var cssProperty =
```

```
            $active.closest('.dial').data('property');
        var cssValue = $active.data('value');

        if (cssProperty && cssValue) {
            $('#textContainer').css(cssProperty, cssValue);
        }
    }
}
/* ]]> */
</h:outputScript>
```

Now, if you scroll the non-window elements over different font sizes, then the content font will be changed immediately.

# Scroll analytics

Waypoint can be used to track the currently focused section of the web page and ad views into the picture when the scroll reaches a certain stage. Waypoint uses the current layout pane as scroll context.

The following XHTML code is used to track user engagement and frontend ad views when it reaches a certain stage:

```
<h:form id="mainForm">
<pe:waypoint id="waypoint1" for="@(.ad-unit)"
      forContext="@(#mainForm .pe-layout-pane-content)"
              offset="'bottom-in-view'" triggerOnce="true">
    <p:ajax event="reached"
        onstart="$(cfg.ext.waypoint).addClass('active')"
            listener="#{waypointController.adInView}"
                update="growl"/>
</pe:waypoint>

<pe:waypoint id="waypoint2" for="container"
    forContext="@(#mainForm .pe-layout-pane-content)"
              offset="function(){return
              $.waypoints('viewportHeight') - $(this).height()}">
    <pe:javascript event="reached" execute="$('#article-
        finished').toggleClass('hiding', ext.direction ===
        'up');"/>
</pe:waypoint>
</h:form>
```

The following JavaScript and CSS script can be used to add styles dynamically in the page:

```
<h:outputScript id="waypointScript" target="body">
/* <![CDATA[ */
    $(document).ready(function() {
        $('body').append($("<div class='ui-widget ui-widget-header
hiding' id='article-finished'>" +
            "Congrats! You have finished reading the articles.</
div>"));
    });
/* ]]> */
</h:outputScript>
<h:outputStylesheet id="waypointCSS">
.ad-unit.active {
        background: #faa7a7;
}

    #article-finished {
        position: fixed;
        z-index: 999;
        bottom: 20px;
        right: 20px;
        padding: 15px;
}

    #article-finished.hiding {
        right: -340px;
}
}
```

Based on the scroll positions, you can customize your web page using the JavaScript and CSS script dynamically.

# JobHub in action

Let us try to apply some of the major features of Waypoint, such as image loading with animation and back to top links, when they reach a certain scroll position. Perform the following steps to do it:

1. Create an XHTML code that contains two Waypoint components. One component can be used to load the images with defined opacity and the other component can be used for back to top functionality. The code is as follows:

```
<pe:waypoint id="waypoint1" offset="'100%'">
    <pe:javascript event="reached"
```

```
        execute="handleWaypoint(ext);" />
</pe:waypoint>
<p:commandButton id="topLink" type="button" value="TOP"
    icon="ui-icon-triangle-1-n" styleClass="top hidden"
    title="Back to top"
    onclick="$('html, body').animate({scrollTop: 0},
    'fast');" />
<pe:waypoint id="waypoint2" offset="'-100%'">
    <pe:javascript event="reached"
        execute="$('.ui-button').toggleClass('hidden');" />
</pe:waypoint>
```

The following JavaScript function is called using ClientBehaviours when the scroll reaches a certain position:

```
<h:outputScript id="waypointScript" target="body">
/* <![CDATA[ */
    function handleWaypoint(ext) {
        var img = $(ext.waypoint);
        // show a smooth animation
        img.css('opacity', 0);
        // change src
        img.attr('src', img.attr('src'));
        // note: call .load() on cached images is not
        reliable.
        // better to use
        https://github.com/desandro/imagesloaded
        img.load(function(){
            img.animate({ opacity: 1 }, 500);
            // remove data-src
            img.removeAttr('data-src');
            // destroy waypoint
            img.waypoint('destroy');
        });
    }
/* ]]> */
</h:outputScript>
```

The following CSS script is attached dynamically during the whole Waypoint functionality:

```
<h:outputStylesheet id="waypointCSS">
    #wrapper {
        width: 560px;
        margin: 0 auto;
    }
```

```
#container {
    margin-bottom: 20px;
}
.top {
    position: fixed;
    right: 20px;
    bottom: 20px;
    font-size: 14px;
    box-shadow: 0 0 15px 1px #808080;
}
.top.hidden {
    display: none;
}
</h:outputStylesheet>

<h:outputStylesheet id="fluidGridCSS">
    img {
        margin-top: -4px;
    }
</h:outputStylesheet>
```

2.  Run the application and navigate to the JobSeeker's **JobsList** screen. Now you click on the company links, which will navigate you to the pages on which the companies are listed using the URL http://localhost:8080/ jobhub/views/companiesList.xhtml.

    If you scroll the page, you see the images loaded with the animation; the **TOP** button appears when the scroller reaches to the end of the page.

Clicking on the **TOP** button scrolls the web page to the top of the screen.

# BlockUI and Spotlight-masking components and their features

Masking components such as BlockUI and Spotlight were introduced to make UIs more attractive and they were controlled by blocking a certain piece of the web page. BlockUI allows certain parts of a page to be blocked using Ajax calls and Spotlight is useful for restricting input to a specific element by masking other parts of the page.

## BlockUI

BlockUI allows blocking any piece of a web page using Ajax calls and makes a transparent blocking layer over the target elements. BlockUI is initiated by the source component to block one or more target elements. You can block a certain part of a page or an entire page by following the convention of wrapping the `div` element (`h:panelGroup` with `layout="block"`) irrespective of working with a few HTML elements, such as `table` or `span`, that cannot be blocked.

BlockUI supports some of the major client-side widget methods as follows:

- `block()`
- `unblock()`

BlockUI components support the following features:

- Common usages
- The autoShown mode and page blocking
- The noncentered messages and auto-unblock

## Common usages

To control the UI during the Ajax calls from either Ajax-supported command actions or ajaxBehavior events, the `block()`/`unblock()` widget methods are called from the JavaScript callback functions.

The most common use case is to block the `dataTable` when events such as sort, filter, and pagination are fired.

The following XHTML code is used to block `dataTable` when `dataTable` sorting and pagination events are fired:

```
<p:dataTable id="dataTable" var="message"
    value="#{dataTableController.messages}" paginator="true"
    paginatorTemplate="{FirstPageLink} {PreviousPageLink}
```

```
    {PageLinks} {NextPageLink} {LastPageLink}
    {RowsPerPageDropdown}"
    rows="5" rowsPerPageTemplate="5,10,15"
    paginatorPosition="bottom">
        <p:ajax event="page"
            onstart="PF('blockUIWidget').block()"
            oncomplete="PF('blockUIWidget').unblock()"/>
        <p:ajax event="sort"
            onstart="PF('blockUIWidget').block()"
            oncomplete="PF('blockUIWidget').unblock()"/>
        <p:column sortBy="subject" headerText="Subject">
            <h:outputText value="#{message.subject}"/>
        </p:column>
        <p:column sortBy="text" headerText="Text">
            <h:outputText value="#{message.text}"/>
        </p:column>
    </p:dataTable>
<pe:blockUI target="dataTable" widgetVar="blockUIWidget">
    <h:panelGrid columns="2">
        <h:graphicImage library="images" name="ajax-loader.gif"/>
        <h:outputText value="Adding message..." />
    </h:panelGrid>
</pe:blockUI>
```

When the event starts firing, you have to call the `block()` method and stop the BlockUI behavior with the `unblock()` method when it is going to complete the Ajax event.

# The autoshown mode and page blocking

You can block the UI for all the Ajax calls without making any explicit calls on the BlockUI component. But you can also limit it for certain Ajax event calls by the use of event attributes. You can specify the list of events separated by a comma for the BlockUI component that acts as a listener.

The following XHTML code contains the BlockUI component that is shown automatically when the page loads:

```
<pe:blockUI source="accessRights" target="@(.blockable)"
    autoShow="true" event="sort,page">
      <h:panelGrid columns="2">
            <h:graphicImage library="images" name="ajax-
                loader.gif" />
            <h:outputText value="Checkbox clicked..." />
      </h:panelGrid>
</pe:blockUI>
```

You can also block the entire page without mentioning the target element. This way, it results in the entire page being blocked. The code to do it is as follows:

```
<p:commandButton value="Block this page!"
  onstart="PF('blockUIWidget').block()"
oncomplete="PF('blockUIWidget').unblock()"/>
<pe:blockUI widgetVar="blockUIWidget">
    <h:panelGrid columns="2">
        <h:graphicImage library="images" name="ajax-loader.gif"/>
        <h:outputText value="Please wait..." />
    </h:panelGrid>
</pe:blockUI>
```

This way, the target can be a component ID, a jQuery/PFS selector, or without the mention of the `target` attribute for entire page blocking.

# The noncentered messages and auto-unblock

You can display a noncentered message with the help of the BlockUI component's CSS, `centerX/centerY` attribute, and `cssOverlay` to style the transparent layer. You can also add a `timeout` attribute for auto-unblock after waiting for some time.

The following XHTML code represents the BlockUI component with custom message position and the auto-unblock feature with the `timeout` property. The `timeout` value will be described in milliseconds.

```
<p:commandButton value="Block this page!" type="button"
                 onclick="PF('blockUIWidget').block()"/>
<pe:blockUI widgetVar="blockUIWidget"
            css="{top: '10px', left: '', right: '10px',
                cursor: 'wait'}"
            cssOverlay="{backgroundColor: 'red'}"
            timeout="3000"
            centerY="false">
    <h:panelGrid columns="2">
        <h:graphicImage library="images" name="ajax-loader.gif" />
        <h:outputText value="This is a non-centered message.
            Please wait..." />
    </h:panelGrid>
</pe:blockUI>
```

# JobHub in action

Let us demonstrate entire page blocking with the BlockUI component when you are trying to register the new employer details as follows:

1. Create the following XHTML code that contains the BlockUI with page scope as target:

```
<p:commandButton value="Register" update=":employerForm"
    global="false"
    actionListener="#{employerDetailsController.
        registerEmployer}"
    onstart="PF('blockUIWidgetPage').block()"
    oncomplete="PF('blockUIWidgetPage').unblock()">
</p:commandButton>
<pe:blockUI widgetVar="blockUIWidgetPage">
    <h:panelGrid columns="2">
    <h:graphicImage value="/resources/images/process/
        ajax-loader.gif"
        style="margin-right: 12px; vertical-align: middle;"
    />
        <h:outputText value="Please wait, data is being
            inserted..." style="white-space: nowrap;" />
    </h:panelGrid>
</pe:blockUI>
```

2. Run the application and navigate to the employer's Employers List page with the URL `localhost:8080/jobhub/views/employerslist.xhtml` using the employer's role.

   Now enter the new employer's details and click on the **Register** button. You then find that BlockUI blocks the entire web page till the event is complete.

Here, you have to call the BlockUI methods on start and on complete callbacks of the command button. You don't need to mention the target for entire page blocking.

# Spotlight

The Spotlight component allows restricting the input to a particular element by masking other parts of the web page. Hence, other parts of the page cannot impact the currently focussed element. Once the current functionality is complete, other parts of the page get activated.

You can use this component with both Ajax behavior and a client-side JavaScript component.

## Ajax behavior support

Wrap the content with the Spotlight component and block the page based on Ajax calls.

The following XHTML code represents the Spotlight component for a particular area of the page:

```
<pe:spotlight id="idPanel"
    blocked="${spotlightController.editable}" >
    //code related to the web page
</pe:spotlight>
```

You can enable or disable the `blocked` property based on the Ajax calls from input commands.

## JavaScript API support

You can use the JavaScript widget API methods, `block()`/`unblock()`, to activate/deactivate the Spotlight component.

The following XHTML code starts and stops the behavior through widget functions such as `block()` and `unblock()`:

```
<pe:spotlight blocked="true" widgetVar="secondSpotlight"
    //Content goes here
      <p:commandButton type="button" value="JS Block" icon="ui-icon-
          locked"
          onclick="PF('secondSpotlight').block()"/>
      <p:commandButton type="button" value="JS Unblock" icon="ui-
          icon-unlocked"
          onclick="PF('secondSpotlight').unblock()"/>
</pe:spotlight>
```

As per the previous code, the Spotlight component is blocked by default and you can change the behavior with client-side widget functions.

# JobHub in action

Let us demonstrate Spotlight's usage in data processing or data inserting areas of application. Perform the following steps:

1.  Create the following XHTML code that contains the Spotlight component to wrap the form components; it is unblocked by default:

```
<p:dialog id="dialog" header="Employer Detail"
    widgetVar="singleEmployerDialog" resizable="false"
    showEffect="fade" hideEffect="explode">
<pe:spotlight id="idPanel1"
    blocked="#{employerDetailsController.editable}"
    style="padding:10px;margin:10px;"
    styleClass="ui-widget ui-widget-content ui-corner-
    all">
    <h:panelGrid id="displaySingle" columns="2"
        cellpadding="4">

    <h:outputText value="Organization Name:" />
    <h:inputText
        value="#{employerDetailsController
        .selectedEmployer.orgname}"
        style="font-weight:bold"
        disabled="#{!employerDetailsController.editable}" />

    <h:outputText value="Branch:" />
    <h:inputText
        value="#{employerDetailsController.selectedEmployer.
        branch}" disabled="#{!employerDetailsController
        .editable}" style="font-weight:bold" />

    <h:outputText value="Established year:" />
    <h:inputText
        value="#{employerDetailsController
        .selectedEmployer.establishedyear}"
        disabled="#{!employerDetailsController
        .editable}" style="font-weight:bold" />

    <h:outputText value="Number of employees:" />
    <h:inputText
        value="#{employerDetailsController
        .selectedEmployer.noofemployees}"
        style="font-weight:bold"
```

```
                disabled="#{!employerDetailsController.editable}" />
        </h:panelGrid>
            <p:selectBooleanButton
                value="#{employerDetailsController.editable}"
                    offLabel="Edit" onLabel="Save">
            <p:ajax event="change" process="idPanel1"
                update="idPanel1,employersList" />
            </p:selectBooleanButton>
    </pe:spotlight>
</p:dialog>
```

2. Run the application and navigate to the employer's **EmployersList** page with the URL `localhost:8080/jobhub/views/employerslist.xhtml` using the employer's role.

   Select any row in which you want to edit the employer details and click on the **Edit** button. Now you can see the pop-up dialog with blocked behavior on form components, as follows:

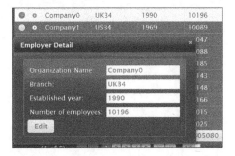

Click on the **Edit** button to enable the form components. Now you can see that, with the exception of the form fields panel, all other remaining content is blocked, as follows:

Once you edit the employer details and click on the **Save** button, results in the form of employer details are listed.

# Summary

In this chapter, you have been introduced to the layout, scroll context, and screen blocking components. These components covered topics such as understanding the layout design components and their features, Waypoint as scroll context components for big data pages, and BlockUI and Spotlight screen-blocking for blocking the web pages.

In the next chapter, we will take a detailed look at the data container and QR code components to provide the master detail hierarchical data relationships, and a cascading grid of items, and also to generate QR codes for marketing products. The major use cases of these components will be explained through development of the JobHub application.

# 4
# The Enriched Data Container and QR Code Components

PrimeFaces core library provided many data container components, such as datatable, subtable, datagrid, and datalist, to accumulate big datasets with lots of features. These components hold iterative data in the form of plain text, images, and other JSF or PrimeFaces UI components' content. The PrimeFaces Extensions team introduced enhanced data container components such as MasterDetail to display multilevel data in order to save web page space and FluidGrid component to display cascading data in addition to the existing data container components developed from the PrimeFaces core library. Apart from the data container components, the Extensions team added a new QR code component as the best alternative to the conventional bar codes.

In this chapter, we will cover the following topics:

- Understanding the MasterDetail component and its various features
- Explaining the FluidGrid cascading component and its features
- Introducing the newly added QR codes and their usages

## Understanding the MasterDetail component and its various features

The MasterDetail component allows us to group data contents into multiple levels and save the web page space for the remaining important areas of the application. The grouped data is maintained in a hierarchical manner and can be navigated through flexible built-in breadcrumbs or command components to go forward and backward in the web interface.

Each level in the content flow is represented by a **MasterDetailLevel** component. This component will hold the PrimeFaces/JSF data iterative or form components inside the grouping components. You can also switch between levels with the help of the **SelectDetailLevel** handler, which is based on Ajax, and dynamically load the levels through Ajax behavior. The SelectDetailLevel handler can be attached to the ajaxified PrimeFaces components and standard JSF components. These components also support the header and footer facets.

The following list of components can be used with the SelectDetailLevel component to support navigations:

- Command actions (CommandButton, commandLink, and remoteCommand)
- MenuItem and HotKey
- Built-in ajaxified components with `p:ajax` or `f:ajax`

The SelectDetailLevel component also controls the partial validation and server-side listener's invocation during the navigations. The areas that need to be updated during the navigations are set automatically in the MasterDetail component, but you can also control them very precisely with the `process` and `update` attributes. If required, you can avoid the partial validations during navigation by setting `process="@none"` or `immediate="true"`. By default, the partial validations are skipped for navigations via breadcrumbs.

If you have any autoupdate components, such as growl or messages, with the `autoUpdate="true"` setting inside the MasterDetail component, then remember to mention the MasterDetail reference in the command component's update attribute.

 The MasterDetail component doesn't work inside the data iteration components, such as datatable, datagrid, and datalist, which extend UIData.

The MasterDetail component supports the following set of features:

- Level-by-level basic navigations
- Wizard-like navigations with forms
- The MasterDetail view with CRUD operations

# Level-by-level basic navigations

Basic level-by-level navigations can be supported by attaching the SelectLevelDetail handler to the command action components. The objects named context values that are passed from one level to the other level need to be configured with the SelectLevelDetail handler and need to match with the `contextVar` attributes of the next level.

The navigations can be handled by adding the level attribute of each MasterDetailLevel component and also the level or step attribute of the SelectDetailLevel component. The step value can be negative and the default value is 1.

You can customize the text of the built-in breadcrumb with the help of the `levelLabel` and `label` attributes of the MasterDetailLevel component. You can also disable the breadcrumb clickable items with the `labelDisabled` attribute.

The following XHTML code creates the MasterDetail component with level-by-level navigations from countries to cities:

```
<pe:masterDetail id="masterDetail" level="#{masterDetailController.
  currentLevel}">

    <pe:masterDetailLevel level="1" levelLabel="countries">
        <p:dataTable id="countries" value="#{masterDetailController.
          countries}" var="country">
          <p:column headerText="Country">
              <p:commandLink value="#{country.name}">
                  <pe:selectDetailLevel contextValue="#{country}"/>
              </p:commandLink>
          </p:column>
          <p:column headerText="Number of countries publishing packt
            books">
              <h:outputText value="#{fn:length(country.
                countriesWithPackPublish)}"/>
          </p:column>
        </p:dataTable>
</pe:masterDetailLevel>

    <pe:masterDetailLevel level="2" contextVar="country"
      levelLabel="Cities under#{country.name} leagues">
        <p:dataTable id="countries" value="#{country.
          countriesWithPacktPublish}" var="city">
          <p:column headerText="Cinty">
              <p:commandLink value="#{city.name}">
                  <pe:selectDetailLevel contextValue="#{city}"/>
              </p:commandLink>
```

```
            </p:column>
            <p:column headerText="PinCode">
                <h:outputText value="#{city.pincode}"/>
            </p:column>
        </p:dataTable>
    </pe:masterDetailLevel>
  <h:panelGrid columns="1">
            <p:commandButton value="Go to counties" icon="ui-icon-
                arrowthickstop-1-w">
                <pe:selectDetailLevel level="1"/>
            </p:commandButton>
        </h:panelGrid>
    </pe:masterDetailLevel>
</pe:masterDetail>
```

# Wizard-like navigations with forms

The MasterDetail component allows wizard-like navigations by replacing the data container components with forms inside MasterDetailLevel. Both the header and footer facets are supported. The header facet allows custom content above the breadcrumb navigation bar, and the footer facet allows custom content below the MasterDetail component.

You can add your own custom content for the title bar and remove the breadcrumb feature with the help of the showBreadCrumb="false" setting.

Create the XHTML code that contains the MasterDetail component with the registration form's wizard navigations, as follows:

```
<pe:masterDetail id="masterDetail" level={masterDetailController.curre
  ntLevel}"showBreadcrumb="false">
    <f:facet name="header">
        <p:messages showDetail="true"/>
        <h:panelGroup layout="block">
            <h:panelGroup styleClass="ui-state-default ui-corner-all
                #{masterDetailController.currentLevel eq 1 ? 'ui-state-
                hover' : ''}">
                <h:outputText value="Personal"/>
            </h:panelGroup>
            <h:panelGroup styleClass="ui-state-default ui-corner-all
                #{masterDetailController.currentLevel eq 2 ? 'ui-state-
                hover' : ''}">
                <h:outputText value="Address"/>
            </h:panelGroup>
```

```
            </h:panelGroup>
    </f:facet>

    <pe:masterDetailLevel level="1">
        <p:panel header="Personal Details">
            <h:panelGrid columns="2">
                <h:outputText value="Firstname: *"/>
                <p:inputText required="true" label="Firstname"
                  value="#{masterDetailController.user.firstname}"/>
                <h:outputText value="Lastname: *"/>
                <p:inputText required="true" label="Lastname"
                  value="#{masterDetailController.user.lastname}"/>
                <h:outputText value="Age: "/>
                <p:inputText value="#{masterDetailController.user.
                  age}"/>
            </h:panelGrid>
        </p:panel>
        <p:commandButton value="Next" process="masterDetail"
            icon="ui-icon-arrowthick-1-e">
            <pe:selectDetailLevel step="1"/>
        </p:commandButton>
        <p:commandButton value="Go to Save" process="masterDetail"
            icon="ui-icon-arrowthickstop-1-e">
            <pe:selectDetailLevel level="2"/>
        </p:commandButton>
    </pe:masterDetailLevel>

    <pe:masterDetailLevel level="2">
        <p:panel header="Adress Details">
            <h:panelGrid columns="2">
                <h:outputText value="Street: "/>
                <p:inputText value="#{masterDetailController.user.
                  street}"/>
                <h:outputText value="Postal Code: "/>
                <p:inputText value="#{masterDetailController.user.
                  postalCode}"/>
                <h:outputText value="City: "/>
                <p:inputText value="#{masterDetailController.user.
                  city}"/>
            </h:panelGrid>
        </p:panel>
        <p:commandButton value="Back" icon="ui-icon-arrowthick-1-w"
```

```
                    process="@this" immediate="true">
            <pe:selectDetailLevel step="-1"/>
        </p:commandButton>
    </pe:masterDetailLevel>
    <p:commandButton value="Submit" process="masterDetail"
        actionListener="#{masterDetailController.save}"
        icon="ui-icon-disk">        </p:commandButton>
    </pe:masterDetailLevel>
</pe:masterDetail>
```

# The MasterDetail view with CRUD operations

You can also create MasterDetail complex views with the combination of CRUD operations and server-side flow listener. The flow listener will be called by passing SelectLevelEvent, and its return value controls the level that needs to be navigated.

Using SelectLevelEvent, you can navigate to the next level or previous levels at any time. If the page validations failed, then you can stay on the same view.

Create the XHTML code that contains the MasterDetail component with all the CRUD operations as follows:

```
<pe:masterDetail id="masterDetail"
selectLevelListener="#{ masterDetailController.handleNavigation}"
                showAllBreadcrumbItems="true">
    <f:facet name="header">
        <p:messages showDetail="false" showSummary="true"/>
    </f:facet>
    <pe:masterDetailLevel level="1">
        <f:facet name="label">
            <h:outputFormat value="Personal Details">
        </f:facet>
        <p:dataTable id="persons" value="#{masterDetailController.
          persons}" var="person">
            <p:column headerText="First Name">
                <p:commandLink value="#{person.firstname}">
                    <pe:selectDetailLevel contextValue="#{person}"/>
                </p:commandLink>
            </p:column>
            <p:column headerText="Last Name">
                <h:outputText value="#{person.lastname}"/>
            </p:column>
            <p:column headerText="Age">
```

```
                <h:outputText value="#{person.age}"/>
            </p:column>
        </p:dataTable>
    </pe:masterDetailLevel>
    <pe:masterDetailLevel level="2" contextVar="person"
      levelLabel="Person Detail">
        <h:panelGrid id="personDetail" columns="2">
            <h:outputText value="First Name"/>
            <p:inputText value="#{person.firstname}" required="true"
              label="First Name"/>
            <h:outputText value="Last Name"/>
            <p:inputText value="#{person.lastname}" required="true"
              label="Last Name"/>
            <h:outputText value="Age"/>
            <p:inputText value="#{person.age}" required="true"
                label="Age">         <p:commandButton value="Save with
                success" process="masterDetail"
                action="#{masterDetailController.saveSuccess(person)}"
                icon="ui-icon-disk">
    <pe:selectDetailLevel level="1"/>
    </p:commandButton>
        <p:commandButton value="Save with failure"
           process="masterDetail" action="#{masterDetailController.
           saveFailure(person)}" icon="ui-icon-disk">
            <pe:selectDetailLevel level="1"/>
        </p:commandButton>
        <p:commandButton type="button" value="Delete" action="#{master
          DetailController.delete(person)}"
    onclick="alert('Are you sure you want to delete this person?')"/>
        </pe:masterDetailLevel>
</pe:masterDetail>
```

You can also control navigations with the flow listener in the server-side Java code as follows:

```java
public int handleNavigation(SelectLevelEvent selectLevelEvent) {
        if (errorOccured) {
            return 2;
        } else {
            return selectLevelEvent.getNewLevel();
        }
    }
```

# JobHub in action

Let us navigate to the JobSeeker's **JobsList** screen using the JobSeeker login and then navigate to multiple levels using either the command links or built-in breadcrumb, if it is available at the top of the MasterDetail component. Now you will see a step-by-step approach to create the MasterDetail component as follows:

1. Create the XHTML code that contains the multilevel data container components inside the MasterDetailLevel component. You can navigate level-by-level from the list of posts and job category to skills details.

```
<h:form id="masterDetailform">
<pe:masterDetail id="masterDetail" level="#{jobDetailsController.
currentLevel}">
  <pe:masterDetailLevel level="1" levelLabel="List of all posts">
    <p:dataTable id="posts" value="#{jobDetailsController.
      jobPosts}"
      var="post" widgetVar="postsWidgetVar" rows="10"
        paginator="true" paginatorPosition="bottom"
        filteredValue="#{jobDetailsController.filteredPosts}" >
      <f:facet name="header">
  <p:inputText id="globalFilter" onkeyup="postsWidgetVar.filter()"
    style="width:150px;display:none;" />
      </f:facet>
      <p:column headerText="Post Title" filterBy="title"
        width="60" filterStyle="display:none;">
    <p:commandLink value="#{post.title}">
     <pe:selectDetailLevel contextValue="#{post}" />
    </p:commandLink>
      </p:column>
      <p:column headerText="Description"
        filterBy="postDescription" width="110"
      filterStyle="display:none;">
      <h:outputText value="#{post.postDescription}" />
      </p:column>
      <p:column headerText="Location" filterBy="location"
        width="20" filterStyle="display:none;width:10px">
    <h:outputText value="#{post.location}" />
      </p:column>
      <p:column headerText="Status"  width="20" filterStyle="displa
        y:none;width:10px">
      <p:selectBooleanButton value="#{post.status}"
        onLabel="Applied"
        offLabel="Apply">
      </p:selectBooleanButton>
      </p:column>
```

```
    </p:dataTable>
  </pe:masterDetailLevel>
  <pe:masterDetailLevel level="2" contextVar="post"
    levelLabel="Jobs related to #{post.title}">
  <p:dataTable id="jobs" value="#{post.jobDetails}" var="job">
  <p:column headerText="Job Category">
     <p:commandLink value="#{job.jobCategory}">
     <pe:selectDetailLevel contextValue="#{job}" />
     </p:commandLink>
  </p:column>
  <p:column headerText="Experience">
     <h:outputText value="#{job.experience}" />
  </p:column>
  <p:column headerText="Position">
    <h:outputText value="#{job.position}" />
  </p:column>
  </p:dataTable>
  </pe:masterDetailLevel>
  <pe:masterDetailLevel level="3" contextVar="job"
  levelLabel="Skills related to #{job.jobCategory}">
     <p:dataTable id="skills" value="#{job.skillsDetails}"
       var="skill">
  <p:column headerText="Frameworks/Technologies">
    <h:outputText value="#{skill.frameworks}" />
  </p:column>
  <p:column headerText="Experience">
    <h:outputText value="#{skill.experience}" />
  </p:column>
        <p:column headerText="Certifications">
    <h:outputText value="#{skill.certifications}" />
  </p:column>
  <p:column headerText="Rating">
    <h:outputText value="#{skill.rating}" />
  </p:column>
    </p:dataTable>
    <h:panelGrid columns="2" style="margin-top: 10px">
  <p:commandButton value="Go to Posts" icon="ui-icon-
    arrowthickstop-1-w">
    <pe:selectDetailLevel level="1" />
  </p:commandButton>
  <p:commandButton value="Go to JobDetails" icon="ui-icon-
    arrowthick-1-w">
    <pe:selectDetailLevel step="-1" />
  </p:commandButton>
```

```
        </h:panelGrid>
      </pe:masterDetailLevel>
    </pe:masterDetail>
  </h:form>
```

2.  Create the MasterDetail component's data container list, such as jobPosts, jobDetails, and skillDetails, in the managed bean code as follows:

```
public class JobDetailsController implements Serializable {
    private static final long serialVersionUID = 20111120L;
    private List<JobPost> jobPosts;
    private int currentLevel = 1;
     public JobDetailsController() {
    jobPosts = new ArrayList<JobPost>();
    loadJobPosts();
    }
public void loadJobPosts(){

    // SrArchitect
    List<JobDetails> JobDetailsArchList = new
ArrayList<JobDetails>();
    JobDetails jobDetails = new JobDetails("Java Domain","10","B11-
Architect", getSkillsDetails("Java"));
    JobDetailsArchList.add(jobDetails);
    jobDetails = new JobDetails(".NET Domain","8","B12-Architect",
getSkillsDetails(".NET"));
    JobDetailsArchList.add(jobDetails);
    jobDetails = new JobDetails("DB Domain","12","A14-Architect",
getSkillsDetails("DB"));
    JobDetailsArchList.add(jobDetails);
    jobDetails = new JobDetails("SAP Domain", "14", "B13-
Architect",  getSkillsDetails("SAP"));
    JobDetailsArchList.add(jobDetails);
    jobPosts.add(new JobPost("SrArchitect","Architectural
designs","US",false, JobDetailsArchList));
    //Other positions goes here
}
private List<SkillsDetails> getSkillsDetails(String title) {
    List<SkillsDetails> skillDetails = new
ArrayList<SkillsDetails>();
    if(title.equalsIgnoreCase("JAVA")){
    skillDetails.add(new SkillsDetails("JSF","10","OCJP","Advanc
ed"));
    skillDetails.add(new SkillsDetails("Spring","8","not
required","Excellant"));
    skillDetails.add(new SkillsDetails("Struts","12","Any","Advanc
ed"));
    //Other skills go here
}
```

3. Run the application and navigate to the `jobsList` page with the browser's URL, `http://localhost:8080/jobhub/views/jobsList.xhtml`, using the JobSeeker's role.

Now, you are able to see the list of all the posts as shown in the following screenshots:

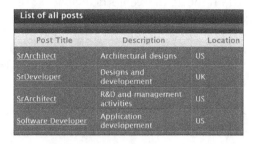

Click on any of the **Post Title** options. This navigates through the jobs related to the position as follows:

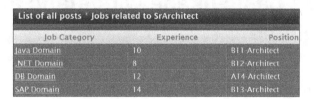

Click on any of the **Job Category** options to populate all the skills or technologies related to it, as shown in the following screenshot:

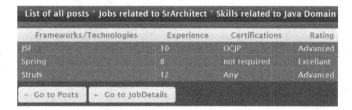

You can also jump to the list of posts and JobDetails section through the navigation bar at the bottom of the screen.

# Explaining the FluidGrid cascading component and its features

FluidGrid creates a grid layout design in a cascading style by placing the elements in an optimal position based on the available vertical space. This sort of mechanism is similar to a mason fitting stones in a wall. According to the window size, the items of FluidGrid are scattered and fit well with the optimal available space.

This component development is based on the **Masonry** JavaScript library and the features that it supports are mentioned as follows:

- FluidGrid's basic usage with static and dynamic items
- Stamped elements within layout and widget functions
- Creating dynamic forms

## FluidGrid's basic usage with static and dynamic items

FluidGrid allows us to set up a layout grid with the items that have variable height and width. This component is more responsive and reflows when the widow resizes. You can place any custom content such as images, links, texts, and input components. The items can be represented in static and dynamic forms as with any iterative components.

You can configure the horizontal and vertical space between the items using the `hGutter` and `vGutter` properties.

### Static items

You can place the static items under the FluidGrid component with the use of the `pe:fluidGridItem` component tag. Based on the number of items available, you may need to place `pe:fluidGridItem` multiple times.

You may have to provide the common style classes for FluidGrid, FluidGridItems containers, and each item style class with variable height and width properties.

For example, in the following sample code, the main container of `pe:fluidGrid` has the `pe-fluidgrid` style class, and the container of `pe:fluidGridItem` has the `pe-fluidgriditem` style class.

The following XHTML code creates the FluidGrid component with static items, with horizontal and vertical space between them:

```
<pe:fluidGrid hGutter="10" vGutter="10">
    <pe:fluidGridItem styleClass="ui-widget-header">Item 1</
        pe:fluidGridItem>
    <pe:fluidGridItem styleClass="ui-widget-header w2 h2">Item 2</
        pe:fluidGridItem>
    <pe:fluidGridItem styleClass="ui-widget-header h3">Item 3</
        pe:fluidGridItem>
</pe:fluidGrid>
```

You can apply the following custom styles to the FluidGrid component for the containers of `FluidGrid` and `FluidGridItem` as follows:

```
<h:outputStylesheet id="fluidGridCSS">
    .pe-fluidgrid {
        max-width: 500px;
    }
    .pe-fluidgrid .pe-fluidgrid-item {
        width:   30px;
        height: 40px;
        border-radius: 6px;
        padding-top: 1em;
        text-align: center;
    }
    .pe-fluidgrid-item.w2 {width: 100px;}
    .pe-fluidgrid-item.w3 {width: 200px;}
    .pe-fluidgrid-item.h2 {height: 100px;}
    .pe-fluidgrid-item.h3 {height: 2000px;}
</h:outputStylesheet>
```

In the preceding code, you can also find the FluidGrid items with different width and height values.

## Dynamic items

You can also add dynamic items to a collection or list of the `FluidGridItem` instances in the server-side Java code and set an optional datatype for the FluidGrid item. This datatype matches with `pe:fluidGridItem` in the XHTML code. The FluidGrid item instances can be any type of data objects, and these instances are accessed in the XHTML code via the `value` attribute and exposed via the `var` attribute of the `pe:fluidGrid` component.

This component supports the `layoutComplete` event, which is fired after the layout of the grid formed with optimal positions is completed.

>  If you are using image content inside the FluidGrid component, then make sure to set `hasImages=true` in order to fix the image overlapping issues caused by unloaded images. If you set the `hasImages` value to true, then the grid layout will be formed after all the images are loaded with proper sizes.

Create the following XHTML code that contains the FluidGrid component with a dynamic collection or a list of `FluidGridItem` instances:

```
<pe:fluidGrid value="#{fluidGridController.images}" var="image"
          fitWidth="true" hasImages="true">
    <p:ajax event="layoutComplete" update="@none"
          listener="#{fluidGridController.fireLayoutComplete}"/>
    <pe:fluidGridItem>
        <h:graphicImage library="images" name="fluidgrid/#{image.
          name}"/>
    </pe:fluidGridItem>
</pe:fluidGrid>
```

Define the list of `FluidGrid` instances in the server-side code to prepare dynamic items for the FluidGrid component as follows:

```
private List<FluidGridItem> images;
@PostConstruct
protected void initialize() {
    images = new ArrayList<FluidGridItem>();
        for (int i = 0; i < 3; i++) {
                images.add(new FluidGridItem(new Image(i + ".png")));
        }
    }
}
```

Now, you can use the images' list as a dynamic list for the FluidGrid component.

# Stamped elements within layout and widget functions

You can also create stamped elements within the layout grid. Stamped elements are special elements that are not laid out by FluidGrid. FluidGrid will layout its items below the stamped elements instead. In order to specify the stamped elements, make sure to use the stamp attribute, which refers to any search expression.

# Widget functions

You can use `unstamp()` and `stamp()` to toggle the stamped elements and `layout()` to reflow the items in a changed layout. You can also call this `layout()` function when the PrimeFaces or Extensions layout resizes events that are fired in order to display the items in optimal positions.

In addition to the item style classes mentioned in the preceding use case, we have to include the stamped item styles along with the `stamp()` and `unstamp()` widget functions, as shown in the following code:

```
<pe:fluidGrid stamp="@(.pe-fluidgrid .stamp)" resizeBound="false"
widgetVar="fluidGridWdgt">
    <div class="stamp"></div>
    <pe:fluidGridItem styleClass="ui-widget-header w1 h1"/>
    <pe:fluidGridItem styleClass="ui-widget-header w2 h2"/>
    </div>
</pe:fluidGrid>
<h:outputScript id="fluidGridScript" target="body">
    isStamped = true;
    function toggleStamped() {
        // stamp or unstamp element
        if (isStamped) {
            PF('fluidGridWdgt').unstamp($(".pe-fluidgrid .stamp").
            get());
        } else {
            PF('fluidGridWdgt').stamp($(".pe-fluidgrid .stamp").
            get());
        }
        isStamped = !isStamped;
    }
</h:outputScript>
<h:outputStylesheet id="fluidGridCSS">
    .pe-fluidgrid .stamp {
        position: absolute;
        right: 25%;
        top: 15px;
        width: 30%;
        height: 40px;
        background: blue;
        border: 5px dotted black;
    }
</h:outputStylesheet>
```

# Creating dynamic forms

You can create dynamic forms with input fields. This is similar to the dynaForm component with dynamically cascading data grid items. After the layout or window is resized, the items will be scattered, and they will fit in an optimal vertical space available. Placing the labels above the input fields is recommended considering the consistency of alignments.

Create the following XHTML code that contains the FluidGrid component with dynamic cascading data grid items as follows:

```
<pe:fluidGrid id="fluidGrid" value="#{fluidGridController.items}"
    var="data" resizeBound="false" hGutter="20"
    widgetVar="fluidGridWdgt">
    <pe:fluidGridItem type="input">
        <div class="dynaFormLabel">
            <p:outputLabel for="txt" value="#{data.label}"/>
        </div>
        <p:inputText id="txt" value="#{data.value}" required="#{data.
            required}"/>
    </pe:fluidGridItem>
    <pe:fluidGridItem type="select" styleClass="select">
        <div class="dynaFormLabel">
            <p:outputLabel for="menu" value="#{data.label}"/>
        </div>
        <p:selectOneMenu id="menu" value="#{data.value}"
            required="#{data.required}">
            <f:selectItems value="#{data.selectItems}"/>
        </p:selectOneMenu>
    </pe:fluidGridItem>
</pe:fluidGrid>
Configure the FluidGrid input fields items similar to DynaForm model.
private List<FluidGridItem> items;
@PostConstruct
protected void initialize() {
    items = new ArrayList<FluidGridItem>();
    List<SelectItem> selectItems = new ArrayList<SelectItem>();
    selectItems.add(new SelectItem("1", "Label 1"));
    selectItems.add(new SelectItem("2", "Label 2"));
    selectItems.add(new SelectItem("3", "Label 3"));
    items.add(new FluidGridItem(new DynamicField("First Label", null,
        true, null), "input"));
```

```
items.add(new FluidGridItem(new DynamicField("Second Label", null,
   false, selectItems),   "select"));
items.add(new FluidGridItem(new DynamicField("Fourth Label", "2",
   false, selectItems),   "select"));
items.add(new FluidGridItem(new DynamicField("Fifth Label", null,
   true, null), "calendar"));
}
Create the dynamic fields with all possible properties as follows
class DynamicField implements Serializable {
    private String label;
    private Object value;
    private boolean required;
    private List<SelectItem> selectItems;
  //getter,setters and constructors
}
```

# JobHub in action

Let us navigate to the company's list screen, which is referenced as a clickable link in the `jobsList` page. Click on the link and navigate to the list of top employers in the grid layout format. Now you will see how to create dynamically cascading items using the FluidGrid component as follows:

1.  Create the XHTML code that contains the FluidGrid component to cascade top employers of the JobHub application as follows:

    ```
    <pe:fluidGrid value="#{employerController.companies}"
      var="company"
                    fitWidth="true" hasImages="true">
     <p:ajax event="layoutComplete" update="@none"
                listener="#{employerController.fireLayoutComplete}"/>
      <pe:fluidGridItem>
          <h:graphicImage id="companyImage" value="/resources/images/
            employers/#{company.name}" >
          <pe:waypoint id="waypoint"    offset="'100%'">
            <pe:javascript event="reached"
              execute="handleWaypoint(ext);"/>
          </pe:waypoint>
          </h:graphicImage>
      </pe:fluidGridItem>
    </pe:fluidGrid>
    ```

2. Create a JSF-managed bean that holds the list of top employers or companies as follows:

```
public class EmployerController implements Serializable {
private List<FluidGridItem> companies;
@PostConstruct
protected void initialize() {
  companies = new ArrayList<FluidGridItem>();
  for (int j = 0; j < 3; j++) {
    for (int i = 0; i <= 16; i++) {
  companies.add(new FluidGridItem(new Company("company"+
    i + ".jpg")));
      }
    }
}
```

3. Run the application and navigate to the `companiesList` page with the browser's `http://localhost:8080/jobhub/views/companiesList.xhtml` URL using the JobSeeker's role.

Now, you are able to see the images that are loaded using the FluidGrid component as follows:

Now, try to resize the window to see the modified cascaded grid items as follows:

Now, the grid items are cascaded based on the optimal vertical space available.

# Newly added QR codes and their usages

QR codes can be used over conventional bar codes to get more benefits that are not provided by bar codes .It can be used in many places, such as to allow the users to browse through websites, initiate phone calls, send e-mails and messages, connect Wi-Fi networks, have access to instant chats, purchase items, process orders, and advertise products.

The Extensions team introduced the QR code component to generate the client-side dynamic QR codes with lots of options such as rendering method, rendering mode, color and size, and so on. This component uses **jQuery.qrcode** behind the scenes.

Create the XHTML code that contains the QR codes with lots of configurable options as follows:

```
<h:panelGrid columns="2">
    <h:outputText value="Render method: " />
    <p:selectOneButton value="#{qrCodeController.renderMethod}">
        <f:selectItem itemLabel="canvas" itemValue="canvas" />
        <f:selectItem itemLabel="image" itemValue="img" />
        <f:selectItem itemLabel="div" itemValue="div" />
    </p:selectOneButton>
    <h:outputText value="Render mode:" />
    <p:selectOneButton value="#{qrCodeController.mode}">
        <f:selectItem itemLabel="normal" itemValue="0" />
        <f:selectItem itemLabel="label strip" itemValue="1" />
        <f:selectItem itemLabel="label box" itemValue="2" />
        <f:selectItem itemLabel="image strip" itemValue="3" />
        <f:selectItem itemLabel="image box" itemValue="4" />
    </p:selectOneButton>
    <h:outputText value="Size:" />
    <h:panelGrid columns="1">
        <h:inputHidden id="size" value="#{qrCodeController.size}" />
        <p:slider minValue="50" maxValue="500" for="size"/>
    </h:panelGrid>
    <h:outputText value="Fill color:" />
    <p:colorPicker value="#{qrCodeController.fillColor}"/>
    <p:commandButton value="update" update="qrCodeElem"/>
</h:panelGrid>
<pe:qrCode id="qrCodeElem" renderMethod="#{qrCodeController.
renderMethod}"
 renderMode="#{qrCodeController.mode}" text="#{qrCodeController.text}"
 label="#{qrCodeController.label}" size="#{qrCodeController.size}"
 fillColor="#{qrCodeController.fillColor}" fontName="Arial"
 fontColor="#DDFF00" ecLevel="H" radius="0.9"/>
```

Now, you can see the generated QR code dynamically with the help of many user controls and options in the following screenshot:

Thus, you can customize the generated QR codes with the help of render method, render mode, size, and fill color options.

# Summary

In this chapter, you have been introduced to the enriched data container components such as MasterDetail for multilevel data, FluidGrid for cascading grid layout, and QR code component for the generation of dynamic QR codes with many options.

In the following chapter, we will take a detailed look at time tracking, schedule components, internationalization support for time-valued registrations, and scheduling/organizing events in universal web applications and their role in the JobHub application development.

# 5
# Time Tracking and Scheduling Components

The PrimeFaces core library provided the calendar and scheduling components to support date and time tracking, scheduling, and manipulating the events and internationalization as some of its main features. To cover many other specific use cases in the modern user interface development, the PrimeFaces Extensions team introduced TimePicker for selecting the time with various types of controls and the TimeLine component as an interactive visualization chart for scheduling new events and manipulating existing events in the long run.

To represent the time in a convenient way with all the possible controls, the Extensions library provided a separate time component to the applications where the time allocation is valuable. The applications such as time registration forms and expense and travel accounts require customized controls with customized time patterns. Although the TimeLine component was introduced as an interactive visualization chart to deal with events tracking and events CRUD operations, both these components support internationalization.

In this chapter, we will cover the following topics:

- Understanding the highly configurable TimePicker component and its features
- The TimeLine component as a visualization chart for CRUD events
- Internationalization support

# Understanding the highly configured TimePicker component and its features

The TimePicker component is a highly customized component to integrate time inputs in both the formats of hours and minutes with user-friendly input controls. The applications where time allocation/selection is mandatory and important, such as time registration, expenses/cost calculation, or travel accounts considering time as the base requirement need a more controlled TimePicker component.

The TimePicker component of the Extensions library developed and provided three divisions of use case features as follows:

- Common basic usages and widget functions
- Advanced usage with events and callback functions
- The time range functionality

## Common basic usages and widget functions

The TimePicker component is available in the following three modes:

- Inline
- Popup
- Spinner

Among all the three modes, spinner is the easiest and most convenient way to represent the time just by increasing and decreasing the values.

You can customize the TimePicker component with a time separator, start and end value for both the hours and minutes, interval for minutes, time period, and the showOn buttons among others.

The following sample syntax represents all the frequently used customizations:

```
<pe:timePicker value="#{timePickerController.time}" mode="popup"
    timeSeparator="-" startHours="8" endHours="20" startMinutes="10"
    endMinutes="40" intervalMinutes="10" showOn="button"
    showCloseButton="true" showDeselectButton="true"
    showNowButton="true" rows="3" showPeriod="true"
    widgetVar="customTimeWidget" label="Custom time picker"/>
```

The spinner mode is not compatible with both the onHourShow and onMinuteShow callbacks, as determining the time with either increment or decrement step by step is not easy.

The TimePicker component also supports the client-side API functions such as enable() and disable().

# Advanced usage with events and callback functions

You can create an advanced TimePicker component with the available Ajax events and callback functions. It supports Ajax events such as timeSelect, beforeShow, and close and callbacks such as the onHourShow and onMinuteShow functions. If you want to use only the hours or minutes panel, then set showMinutes to false or showHours to false in the respective order.

The two callbacks, onHourShow and onMinuteShow, can be used to enable or disable certain hours and minutes respectively.

The following sample syntax represents the advanced TimePicker components that are created with the various events and the callback functions:

```
<pe:timePicker id="inlineTime"
  value="#{timePickerController.time1}" mode="inline">
  <p:ajax event="timeSelect"
    listener="#{timePickerController.timeSelectListener}"/>
  <p:ajax event="beforeShow"
    listener="#{timePickerController.beforeShowListener}"/>
  <p:ajax event="close"
    listener="#{timePickerController.closeListener}" />
</pe:timePicker>
<pe:timePicker value="#{timePickerController.time2}"
  onHourShow="onHourShowCallback"
    onMinuteShow="onMinuteShowCallback"/>
```

In the preceding code, the three listeners, timeSelectListener, beforeShowListener, and closeListener, receive the timeSelect, beforeShow, and close events respectively.

Add the following JavaScript code, which contains the `onHourShow` and `onMinuteShow` callback functions used for the TimePicker component, to the preceding code snippet:

```
<h:outputScript id="timeRangeScript" target="body">
/* <![CDATA[ */
functiononHourShowCallback(hour) {
        if ((hour > 15) || (hour < 3)) {
            return false; // not valid
        }
        return true; // valid
    }
functiononMinuteShowCallback(hour, minute) {
        if ((hour == 15) && (minute >= 15)) {
            return false; // not valid
        }
        if ((hour == 3) && (minute < 15)) {
            return false; // not valid
        }
        return true;  // valid
    }
}
```

## The time range

Sometimes, you may need to select the TimePicker components in a chronological time range. The common use case validation such as the start time should always be less than the end time, which can be achieved with the time range feature implementation.

The following sample syntax of XHTML code creates the time range between the two TimePicker components as follows:

```
<h:panelGrid columns="5">
    <h:outputText value="Start time"/>
    <pe:timePicker value="#{timePickerController.time1}"
  mode="popup" onHourShow="startOnHourShowCallback"
  onMinuteShow="startOnMinuteShowCallback"
  widgetVar="startTimeWidget"/>
    <h:outputText value="End time"/>
    <pe:timePicker value="#{timePickerController.time2}"
  mode="popup" onHourShow="endOnHourShowCallback"
   onMinuteShow="endOnMinuteShowCallback"
  widgetVar="endTimeWidget"/>
</h:panelGrid>
```

The following JavaScript code contains the `onHourShow` and `onMinuteShowCallback` functions to create the time range validation between two TimePicker components:

```
<h:outputScript id="timeRangeScript" target="body">
/* <![CDATA[ */
functionstartOnHourShowCallback(hour) {
        if (!PrimeFaces.widgets['endTimeWidget']) {
            return false;
        }
varendHour = parseInt(PF('endTimeWidget').getHours());
        if (parseInt(hour) <= endHour) {
            return true;
        }
        return false;
    }
functionstartOnMinuteShowCallback(hour, minute) {
        if (!PrimeFaces.widgets['endTimeWidget']) {
            return false;
        }
varendHour = parseInt(PF('endTimeWidget').getHours());
varendMinute = parseInt(PF('endTimeWidget').getMinutes());
        if (parseInt(hour) < endHour) {
            return true;
        }
        if ((parseInt(hour) == endHour) && (parseInt(minute) <
          endMinute)) {
            return true;
        }
        return false;
    }
functionendOnHourShowCallback(hour) {
        if (!PrimeFaces.widgets['startTimeWidget']) {
            return false;
        }
varstartHour = parseInt(PF('startTimeWidget').getHours());
        if (parseInt(hour) >= startHour) {
            return true;
        }
        return false;
    }

functionendOnMinuteShowCallback(hour, minute) {
        if (!PrimeFaces.widgets['startTimeWidget']) {
            return false;
```

```
            }
    varstartHour = parseInt(PF('startTimeWidget').getHours());
    varstartMinute = parseInt(PF('startTimeWidget').getMinutes());
            if (parseInt(hour) > startHour) {
                return true;
            }
            if ((parseInt(hour) == startHour) && (parseInt(minute) >
                startMinute)) {
                return true;
            }
            return false;
        }
    /* ]]> */
    </h:outputScript>
```

# JobHub in action

Let us navigate to the **Professional** tab under the JobSeeker's registration form and fill the available interview timings using the TimePicker components as shown in the following steps:

1.  Create an XHTML code as follows that contains the TimePicker components:

    ```
    <h:outputText value="Preferred Interview Timings-Start: " />
        <pe:timePicker
          value="#{employeeRegistration.jobseeker.interviewFromTime}"
          timeSeparator="-" startHours="9" endHours="12"
          startMinutes="5" endMinutes="55" intervalMinutes="5"
          showCloseButton="true" showDeselectButton="true"
          showNowButton="true" rows="2" showPeriod="true"
          style="width:70px;" widgetVar="customTimeWidget"
          label="Custom time picker" />
        <h:outputText value="End:" />
        <pe:timePicker value="#{employeeRegistration.jobseeker.
          interviewToTime}"
          timeSeparator="-" startHours="13" endHours="16"
          startMinutes="5" endMinutes="55" intervalMinutes="5"
          showCloseButton="true"
          showDeselectButton="true" showNowButton="true" rows="2"
          showPeriod="true" style="width:70px;" label="Custom time
          picker" />
    ```

2.  Create the JSF managed bean with the `jobseeker` instance and define all the properties in POJO.

3.  Run the application and navigate to the JobSeeker's registration page at `http://localhost:8080/jobhub/views/employeeRegistration.xhtml` using the JobSeeker's role.

Now you are able to see the TimePicker component while selecting the start time as shown in the following screenshot:

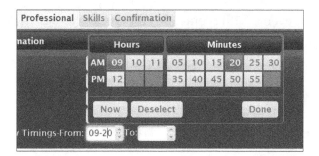

Click on the end time to see the TimePicker component as shown in the following screenshot:

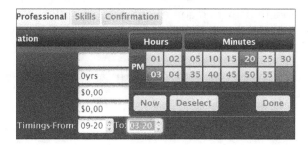

# Managing events using the TimeLine component

TimeLine is an interactive visualization chart for scheduling and manipulating the events in a certain period of time. The time axis scale can be auto-adjusted and ranges from milliseconds to years. The events can take place on a single date or a particular date range.

The TimeLine component supports many features such as read only events, editable events, grouping events, client-side and server-side API, and drag-and-drop.

The Timeline features are divided into the following use cases:

- Common basic usages
- The editable events with client-side API and server-side API
- Grouping and events that can be merged
- Customized styles and internationalization support
- Limit range
- Linked TimeLine components
- Lazy loading events
- Drag-and-drop items

# Common basic usages

The TimeLine component provided some configurable options that are used for any basic TimeLine development. You can change these options dynamically using command actions.

The following are the configurable options or attributes that are listed for creating a basic TimeLine component:

- `selectable`: This defines whether events are selectable or not. Selectable events fire Ajax `"select"` events. The default value is `true`.

- `unselectable`: This defines whether you need to unselect the selected items by clicking outside the events located. The default value is `true`.

- `zoomable`: This defines whether the events are zoomable or not. When the TimeLine component is zoomed, Ajax `rangechange` events are fired. The default value is `true`.

- `movable`: This defines whether the events are movable or not. When the TimeLine component is moved, Ajax `rangechange` events are fired. The default value is `true`.

- `eventStyle`: This defines the styles for the TimeLine events. The possible values for `eventstyle` are `"dot"` and `"box"`. The default value is `box`.

- `axisOnTop`: This defines whether the TimeLine axis is defined at the top of the TimeLine component or not. The default is `false`.

- `showCurrentTime`: This defines whether the red vertical line is displayed with current time. The default value is `true`.

- `showNavigation`: This defines whether the navigation button bar is shown with zoom and movable buttons. The default value is `false`.

Now, let us try to apply the preceding configurable options to the TimeLine component in a step-by-step manner.

Create the following XHTML code that contains all the possible TimeLine configurable options as component attributes:

```
<pe:timeline id="timeline" value="#{timelineController.model}"
    selectable="false" zoomable="false" moveable="false"
    stackEvents="false" axisOnTop="true" eventStyle="dot"
    showCurrentTime="false" showNavigation="true">
    <p:ajax event="select"
      listener="#{timelineController.onSelectListener}"/>
</pe:timeline>
```

Create a TimeLine model that is accessed through the `value` attribute of the TimeLine component in the following XHTML code:

```
privateTimelineModel model;
@PostConstruct
protected void initialize() {
  model = new TimelineModel();
  Calendar cal = Calendar.getInstance();
  cal.set(2014, Calendar.NOV, 25, 0, 0, 0);
  model.add(new TimelineEvent("JobHub Product 1.0",
    cal.getTime()));
  cal.set(2012, Calendar.DEC,10, 0, 0, 0);
  model.add(new TimelineEvent("JobHub Product 2.0",
    cal.getTime()));
  cal.set(2012, Calendar.JANUARY, 12, 0, 0, 0);
  model.add(new TimelineEvent("JobHub Product 3.0",
    cal.getTime()));
  cal.set(2012, Calendar.FEB, 17, 0, 0, 0);
  model.add(new TimelineEvent("JobHub Product 4.0",
    cal.getTime()));
}
public void onSelect(TimelineSelectEvent e) {
  TimelineEventtimelineEvent = e.getTimelineEvent();
}
```

# Editable events with the client-side and server-side APIs

The TimeLine events can be created, content-edited, time-changed, or deleted using either the client-side or server-side API. To proceed with editable events, first you have to enable the `selectable` attribute and then enable the `editable` attribute. The global editable setting can be overwritten by using the individual event's editable property field of the TimeLine modal class.

## How to perform editable events in the user interface

The editable TimeLine fires the Ajax events named `add`, `select`, `edit`, `change`, and `delete` that are explained as follows:

- `add`: Add an event by clicking on the add button in the navigation bar that is visible through setting `showButtonNew=true`, by double-clicking on the TimeLine, or by keeping the *Ctrl* key pressed and clicking on or dragging in the TimeLine

- `select`: Select an event and drag it to another time

- `edit`: Edit the event by double clicking on the contents of the event

- `change`: Select the date range events; it has a drag area on the left side and right side to change the start and end time

- `delete`: Delete the event by clicking on the delete icon that is placed at the top–right corner of the event box.

## The client-side API

The editable events can be manipulated by using the client-side API methods. The most used event manipulation methods are `addItem()`, `changeItem()`, and `deleteItem()`, whereas the respective methods are cancelled by the `cancelAdd()`, `cancelChange()`, and `cancelDelete()` methods. You can also set the `readOnly` events by setting them on an individual basis in the TimeLine modal class as shown in the following code snippet:

```
<pe:timeline id="timeline" widgetVar="timelineWdgt"
  value="#{timelineController.model}"
    editable="true" showButtonNew="true"
      timeZone="#{timelineController.timeZone}">
  <pe:javascript event="add"
    execute="PF('timelineWdgt').addItem();"/>
```

```
        <pe:javascript event="delete"
          execute="PF('timelineWdgt').cancelDelete();"/>
    </pe:timeline>
    <p:commandButton value="Submit" type="button"
                     onclick="updateData(PF('timelineWdgt').getData())"/>
    <p:commandButton value="Show updated timeline model"
      process="@none" update="timeline"
        title="Check if the model has been updated"/>
    <pe:remoteCommand id="updateDataRemote" name="updateData"
      process="@this" actionListener="#{timelineController.updateData}">
        <pe:methodSignature parameters="java.util.List"/>
        <pe:methodParam name="events">
            <pe:convertTimelineEvents/>
        </pe:methodParam>
    </pe:remoteCommand>
    <p:confirmDialog message="Are you sure you want to delete the
        selected event?" header="Delete confirmation" appendTo="@(body)"
        severity="alert" widgetVar="confirmWdgt">
        <p:commandButton value="Delete" type="button"
          onclick="PF('confirmWdgt').hide();
          PF('timelineWdgt').deleteItem();"/>
        <p:commandButton value="Cancel" type="button"
          onclick="PF('confirmWdgt').hide()"/>
    </p:confirmDialog>
```

In this code example, we applied the client-side API methods such as addItem and deleteItem to add a new item and delete the existing item in the given TimeLine range.

# The server-side API

The TimeLine component supports a very convenient server-side API to update the events smoothly. You have to use the Ajax events such as add, edit, change, and delete to get TimelineEvent in the server side and TimelineUpdater for updating a model with new or modified events. The server-side approach reduces the DOM update on the complex UI and avoids UI flickers by making a single request instead of two requests. If you use client-side approach with the update() method, it creates two requests, one request for the actual add or edit operation and other one for updating the UI.

The approach for editing events is similar to the PrimeFaces schedule component but the schedule component uses the client-side API `update()` method for updating itself on the `oncomplete` js callback function, whereas TimeLine uses `TimelineUpdater` for updating the model.

The TimeLine UI updates the server side and an update request for a particular event is sent immediately. The main steps to follow for updating the events are:

1.  Get the `TimelineUpdater` instance using the TimeLine component ID.
2.  Invoke one or more CRUD event operations on `TimelineModel` by passing the `TimelineUpdater` instance as a parameter.

 All the CRUD operations are performed on the `TimelineModel` instance without using the `TimelineUpdater` instance at all. But you have to manually update the model to effect the changes.

The following XHTML code enables the CRUD operations in the TimeLine component using the server-side API:

```
<pe:timeline id="timeline" value="#{timelineController.model}"
  var="task"
  timeZone="#{timelineController.timeZone}"
  zoomMax="#{timelineController.zoomMax}"
  start="#{timelineController.start}"
  end="#{timelineController.end}"
  editable="true" showButtonNew="true"
  widgetVar="timelineWdgt">
    <p:ajax event="change" update="@none"
      listener="#{timelineController.onChange}"/>
    <p:ajax event="edit" update=":eventsdata"
      listener="#{timelineController.onEdit}"
      oncomplete="PF('$eventsdlg').show()"/>
    <p:ajax event="add" update=":eventsdata"
      listener="#{timelineController.onAdd}"
      oncomplete="PF('$eventsdlg').show()"/>
    <p:ajax event="delete" update=":eventsdata"
      listener="#{timelineController.onDelete}"
      onstart="PF('timelineWdgt').cancelDelete()"
        oncomplete="alert('Are you ready to delete event')"/>
        <h:outputText value="Title: #{task.title}"/>
</pe:timeline>
<p:dialog id="eventsDlg" header="Event Details"
  widgetVar="$eventsdlg">
        <h:outputText value="Title"/>
```

```
        <p:inputText
          value="#{timelineController.event.data.title}"/>
          <h:outputText value="Start date"/>
    <p:calendar value="#{timelineController.event.startDate}"
        timeZone="#{timelineController.timeZone}"
        pattern="dd/MM/yyyyHH:mm" required="true" />
  <h:outputText value="End date"/>
        <p:calendar value="#{timelineController.event.endDate}"
        timeZone="#{timelineController.timeZone}"
        pattern="dd/MM/yyyyHH:mm"/>
    <p:commandButton value="Save" process="eventsDlg"
      update="@none"
        action="#{timelineController.saveDetails}"
</p:dialog>
```

You can retrieve the TimeLine events generated by the Ajax events and update the UI on the server side using `TimelineUpdater`.

For example, to enable the add events in the TimeLine component, the managed bean contains the Ajax listener as shown in the following code snippet:

```
public void onAdd(TimelineAddEvent e) {
  event = new TimelineEvent(e.getData(), e.getStartDate(),
    e.getEndDate(), true, e.getGroup());
}
public void saveDetails() {
  TimelineUpdatertimelineUpdater =
    TimelineUpdater.getCurrentInstance(":timeline");
  model.update(event, timelineUpdater);
}
```

In this code example, the organized event details such as event title and start and end date are updated through Ajax events named add, delete, and edit and changed by interacting with the TimeLine model using their respective listener methods.

# Grouping and events that can be merged

You can create all events under the same group as a single vertical line to represent the multiple groups. Grouping events is quite useful to represent multiple items next to each other. The grouped events will not be stacked if they overlap each other, but you can move the editable grouped events. You need to make sure to set `groupsChangeable` so that the events can be moved from one group to other.

You can also merge the events when they get overlapped by dragging and dropping. The TimelineModel instance represents all the necessary methods for getting the overlapped events and merging them with a given event.

In this use case, TimelineUpdater also can be used to update the UI on the server side.

The following XHTML code creates the TimeLine component with the events that can be grouped and merged:

```
<pe:timeline id="timeline" value="#{timelineController.model}"
  var="task"
      editable="true" eventMargin="6" eventMarginAxis="0"
      showMajorLabels="false" axisOnTop="true"
      groupsChangeable="true" groupsOnRight="false"
      timeZone="America/New_York" widgetVar="timelineWdgt">
    <p:ajax event="change" update="@none"
      listener="#{timelineController.onChange}"/>
    <p:ajax event="delete" update="@none"
      listener="#{timelineController.onDelete}"/>
    <p:ajax event="add" update="@none"
      onstart="PF('timelineWdgt').cancelAdd()"/>
    <h:outputText value="Task #{task.title}"/>
</pe:timeline>
// Dialog with overlapped timeline events
<p:dialog id="overlapEventsDlg" header="Overlapped tasks"
  widgetVar="overlapEventsWdgt">
    <h:panelGroup id="overlappedTasks" layout="block" >
      Please choose tasks you want to merge with the task
        #{timelineController.selectedTask}
    <p:selectManyMenu id="overlappedTask"
      value="#{timelineController.tasksToMerge}"
                showCheckbox="true">
      <f:selectItems
        value="#{groupingTimelineController.overlappedTasks}"
        var="task"
        itemLabel=" Task #{task.data.title}" itemValue="#{task}"
          converter="taskconverter"/>
    </p:selectManyMenu>
  </h:panelGroup>
    <f:facet name="footer">
      <p:commandButton value="Merge" process="overlapEventsDlg"
        update="@none"
        action="#{timelineController.merge}"
```

```
                          oncomplete="PF('overlapEventsWdgt').hide()"/>
            <p:commandButton type="button" value="Close"
              onclick="PF('overlapEventsWdgt').hide()"/>
          </f:facet>
      </p:dialog>
```

The following server-side Java code is used to get overlapped tasks and merge
the tasks:

```
//Get the overlapped tasks
public void onChange(TimelineModificationEvent e) {
  event = e.getTimelineEvent();
  model.update(event);
  TreeSet<TimelineEvent> overlappedEvents =
    model.getOverlappedEvents(event);
  if (overlappedEvents == null) {
    return;
  }
   overlappedTasks = new
    ArrayList<TimelineEvent>(overlappedEvents);
  tasksToMerge = null;
}
// merge the tasks
public void merge() {
  // merge tasks which are selected
  if (tasksToMerge != null && !tasksToMerge.isEmpty()) {
    model.merge(event, tasksToMerge,
      TimelineUpdater.getCurrentInstance(":timeline"));
  }
  overlappedTasks = null;
  tasksToMerge = null;
}
```

# The range limit

You can limit the TimeLine range in the following form:

- Minimum visible date

- Maximum visible date

- Minimum visible interval

- Maximum visible interval

To configure the preceding features, you have to use the attributes named `min`, `max`, `zoomMin`, and `zoomMax`. The values of `min` and `max` should be of the `date` type, whereas those of `zoomMin` and `zoomMax` should be of the `long` type in milliseconds.

The following XHTML code represents the TimeLine range with configurable options:

```
<pe:timeline value="#{timelineController.model}"
min="#{timelineController.min}" max="#{timelineController.
max}"zoomMin="#
  {timelineController.zoomMin}"zoomMax="#
  {timelineController.zoomMax}"
showNavigation="true"/>
```

# Linked TimeLine components

You can create linked TimeLines by moving or zooming one TimeLine component, while the other one also gets moved or zoomed. Also, an event selected on one TimeLine can select the event on another TimeLine.

When moving or zooming one TimeLine, you can then get the visible range of it using a `rangechange` event so that you can set the same visible range for the second Timeline.

A visual section can be achieved by either calling `select(TimeLineEvent,TimelineUpdater)` on the `TimelineModel` instance or by calling the `select(int index)` method on the `TimelineUpdater` instance; here `index` refers to the order of the selected events in the events list.

The following XHTML code creates linked TimeLines using two TimeLine components:

```
<pe:timeline id="timelineFirst"
  value="#{timelineController.firstModel}" var="task"
  widgetVar="timelineFirstWdgt">
  <pe:javascript event="rangechange"
    execute="onrangechangeFirst()"/>
    <p:ajax event="select"
      listener="#{linkedTimelinesController.onSelect}"/>
    <h:panelGroup layout="block">
      <h:outputText value="#{task.title}"/>
    </h:panelGroup>
    <p:graphicImage library="images" name="#{task.imagePath}"/>
</pe:timeline>
<pe:timeline id="timelineSecond"
  value="#{linkedTimelinesController.secondModel}"
```

```
    widgetVar="timelineSecondWdgt">
      <pe:javascript event="rangechange"
        execute="onrangechangeSecond()"/>
  </pe:timeline>
```

The following server-side Ajax listener updates the selected events with
TimelineUpdater:

```
// Select the events
public void onSelect(TimelineSelectEvent e) {
  TimelineUpdatertimelineUpdater =
    TimelineUpdater.getCurrentInstance(":timelineSecond");
    if (aSelected) {
      timelineUpdater.select(1);
    } else {
      timelineUpdater.select(0);
    }
  aSelected = !aSelected;
}
```

The following JavaScript functions set the visible range on both the TimeLines:

```
// JavaScript calls for rangechange events
<h:outputScript id="timelineJS" target="body">
/* <![CDATA[ */
$(function() {
  onrangechangefirst();
});
function onrangechange1() {
  var range = PF('timelineFirstWdgt').getVisibleRange();
  PF('timelineSecondWdgt').setVisibleRange(range.start,
    range.end);
}
function onrangechange2() {
  var range = PF('timelineSecondWdgt').getVisibleRange();
  PF('timelineFirstWdgt').setVisibleRange(range.start, range.end);
}
/* ]]> */
</h:outputScript>
```

# Lazy loading events

TimeLine supports lazy loading during the moving or zooming in of the TimeLine components when loading of the events is really time-consuming. Events are lazy-loaded when you attach p:ajax with event="lazyload" to the TimeLine component. The TimelineLazyLoadEvent event class contains one or two time ranges; two ranges will occur when you zoom out the TimeLine component.

You can also use the preloadFactor attribute when lazy loading is active. When you are moving or zooming the TimeLine, the additional time range is added by the multiplication of the calculated time range of preloading with preloadFactor .This avoids the time-consuming fetching of events frequently.

>  The lazy loading listener won't be invoked when the visible range area already has lazy loading events.

The following XHTML code performs the lazy loading of the TimeLine components when moving or zooming the TimeLine components:

```
<pe:timeline id="timeline" value="#{timelineController.model}"
    preloadFactor="#{timelineController.preloadFactor}"
    zoomMax="#{timelineController.zoomMax}" showNavigation="true">
  <p:ajax event="lazyload" update="@none"
    listener="#{timelineController.onLazyLoad}"/>
</pe:timeline>
<h:panelGrid columns="2" style="margin-top:15px">
  <p:spinner id="spinner"
    value="#{lazyTimelineController.preloadFactor}"
      min="0" max="1" stepFactor="0.05"/>
  <p:commandButton value="Update Preload Factor" process="@this
    spinner" update="timeline"
    action="#{timelineController.clearTimeline}"/>
</h:panelGrid>
```

The following server-side code contains the lazy loading Ajax listener for generating the events lazily:

```
//generate lazy load events
public void onLazyLoad(TimelineLazyLoadEvent e) {
TimelineUpdatertimelineUpdater = TimelineUpdater.getCurrentInstance(":
form:timeline");
        Date startDate = e.getStartDateFirst();
        Date endDate = e.getEndDateFirst();
        // moving-fetch events for the first time range
```

```
        generateRandomEvents(startDate, endDate, timelineUpdater);
        // zooming out-fetch events for the second time range
        if (e.hasTwoRanges()) {
            generateRandomEvents(e.getStartDateSecond(),
    e.getEndDateSecond(), timelineUpdater);
        }
    }
public void clearTimeline() {
        model.clear();
    }
```

# Drag-and-drop items

TimeLine supports drag-and-drop features by dragging and dropping the items into the TimeLine component from the outside list. You can activate the drag-and-drop feature by attaching p:ajax with event="drop", and the Ajax listener gets the instance of the TimeLineDragDrop event class.

When the event is dragged and dropped on the timeline, the end date is calculated by the default algorithm that is used in most of the cases.

*End date = start date + 10% of TimeLine width*

You can choose the target time zone and browser time zone with the help of the TimeLine attributes timeZone and browserTimeZone respectively. The target time zone is needed to show the event's start or end dates in TimeLine, whereas the browser time zone is required for correction of the displayed time. Automatic calculation of the browser time zone is not supported due to big JavaScript file sizes.

The following XHTML code creates the TimeLine component that supports drag-and-drop features:

```
<pe:timeline id="timeline" value="#{timelineController.model}"
  var="event"
  editable="true"start="#{timelineController.start}
    "end="#{timelineController.end}
    "timeZone="#{timelineController.targetTZ}"
    browserTimeZone="#{timelineController.browserTZ}"
      dropActiveStyleClass="ui-state-highlight"
        dropHoverStyleClass="ui-state-hover">
    <p:ajax event="drop" listener="#{timelineController.onDrop}"
      global="false" update="eventsList"/>
    <h:panelGrid columns="1">
```

```
      <h:outputText value="#{event.name}"/>
      <h:outputText value="#{event.start}">
        <f:convertDateTimedateStyle="short" type="both"
          timeZone="#{timelineController.targetTZ}"/>
      </h:outputText>
      <h:outputText value="#{event.end}">
        <f:convertDateTimedateStyle="short" type="both"
          timeZone="#{timelineController.localTZ}"/>
      </h:outputText>
    </h:panelGrid>
</pe:timeline>
<h:panelGrid columns="2" >
    <h:outputText value="Choose your target time zone"/>
    <p:selectOneMenu value="#{timelineController.localTZ}">
      <f:selectItems value="#{timelineController.timeZones}"/>
        <p:ajax update="timeline"
          listener="#{timelineController.onSwitchTimeZone}"/>
    </p:selectOneMenu>
    <h:outputText value="Choose your browser's time zone"/>
    <p:selectOneMenu value="#{timelineController.browserTZ}">
      <f:selectItems value="#{timelineController.timeZones}"/>
        <p:ajax update="timeline"
          listener="#{timelineController.onSwitchTimeZone}"/>
    </p:selectOneMenu>
</h:panelGrid>
```

# Internationalization support

Both the TimePicker and TimeLine components support **Internationalization (I18N)** to display localized text or labels. PrimeFaces Extensions only provides English locales. If you want to support multiple locales for multilanguage applications, then you need to add the locales with corresponding text in a JavaScript file and add it to your application. Based on the locale you selected, the corresponding text will be displayed for the component.

For example, add the following TimePicker and TimeLine locale JavaScript files in your application's resources folder to support French local text:

1. Create the timepickerLocales.js file under the resources folder of your application with the following content:

   ```
   $(function() {
     PrimeFacesExt.locales.TimePicker['fr'] = {
       hourText: 'Heures',
       minuteText: 'Minutes',
   ```

```
    amPmText: ['AM', 'PM'],
    closeButtonText: 'Fermer',
    nowButtonText: 'Maintenant',
    deselectButtonText: 'Désélectionner'
    };
}
```

2. Create the `timelineLocales.js` file under the `resources` folder of your application with the following content:

```
$function(){
    PrimeFacesExt.locales.Timeline['fr'] = {
        'MONTHS': ["Janvier", "Février", "Mars", "Avril", "Mai",
            "Juin", "Juillet", "Août", "Septembre", "Octobre",
            "Novembre", "Décembre"],
        'MONTHS_SHORT': ["Jan", "Fev", "Mar", "Avr", "Mai", "Jun",
            "Jul", "Aou", "Sep", "Oct", "Nov", "Dec"],
        'DAYS': ["Dimanche", "Lundi", "Mardi", "Mercredi", "Jeudi",
            "Vendredi", "Samedi"],
        'DAYS_SHORT': ["Dim", "Lun", "Mar", "Mer", "Jeu", "Ven",
            "Sam"],
        'ZOOM_IN': "Zoomer",
        'ZOOM_OUT': "Dézoomer",
        'MOVE_LEFT': "Déplacer à gauche",
        'MOVE_RIGHT': "Déplacer à droite",
        'NEW': "Nouveau",
        'CREATE_NEW_EVENT': "Créer un nouvelévènement"
    };
}
```

# JobHub in action

Let us navigate to the admin page screen using the admin role and then click on the **Jobhub Timeline** tab to track the JobHub posts over the past few years and apply the following CRUD operations:

1. Create the following XHTML code, which contains the editable server-side API of the TimeLine component:

```
<pe:timeline id="timeline"
    value="#{jobhubTimelineController.model}"
    var="jobhub"
    selectable="#{jobhubTimelineController.selectable}"
    zoomable="#{jobhubTimelineController.zoomable}"
    moveable="#{jobhubTimelineController.moveable}"
    stackEvents="#{jobhubTimelineController.stackEvents}"
```

```
axisOnTop="#{jobhubTimelineController.axisOnTop}"
eventStyle="#{jobhubTimelineController.eventStyle}"
showCurrentTime="#{jobhubTimelineController.showCurrentTime
}"
showNavigation="#{jobhubTimelineController.showNavigation}"
timeZone="#{jobhubTimelineController.timeZone}"
zoomMax="#{jobhubTimelineController.zoomMax}"
start="#{jobhubTimelineController.start}"
end="#{jobhubTimelineController.end}" editable="true"
showButtonNew="true" minHeight="200"
  widgetVar="timelineWdgt">

<p:ajax event="change" update="@none"
  listener="#{jobhubTimelineController.onChange}" />
<p:ajax event="edit"
  update="detailsJobhubInner"listener="#
  {jobhubTimelineController.onEdit}"
  oncomplete="PF('detailsJobhubWdgt').show()" />
<p:ajax event="add" update="detailsJobhubInner"
  listener="#{jobhubTimelineController.onAdd}"
  oncomplete="PF('detailsJobhubWdgt').show()" />
<p:ajax event="delete" update="deleteJobhubInner"
  listener="#{jobhubTimelineController.onDelete}"
  onstart="PF('timelineWdgt').cancelDelete()"
    oncomplete="PF('deleteJobhubWdgt').show()" />
    <h:panelGrid columns="1">
      <h:outputText value="Posts: #{jobhub.noofposts}" />
      <h:outputText value="Employers:
        #{jobhub.noofemployers}" />
      <h:outputText value="AppliedPosts:
        #{jobhub.noofappliedposts}" />
    </h:panelGrid>
</pe:timeline>
  <p:dialog id="detailsJobhubDlg" header="Jobhub Details"
    widgetVar="detailsJobhubWdgt" showEffect="clip"
      hideEffect="clip">
    <h:panelGroup id="detailsJobhubInner" layout="block">
      <h:panelGrid columns="2"
        columnClasses="JobhubDetails1,JobhubDetails2">
        <h:outputText value="Posts" />
        <p:inputText value="#{jobhubTimelineController
          .event.data.noofposts}"
            required="true" label="Room" />
```

```
<h:outputText value="Start" />
<p:calendar value="#
  {jobhubTimelineController.event.startDate}"
  timeZone="#{jobhubTimelineController.timeZone}"
  pattern="dd/MM/yyyyHH:mm" required="true" label="From"
    />
<h:outputText value="End" />
<p:calendar value="#{jobhubTimelineController.event.
  endDate}"
  timeZone="#{jobhubTimelineController.timeZone}"
  pattern="dd/MM/yyyyHH:mm" label="Until" />

<h:outputText value="Employers" />
<p:inputText value="#
  {jobhubTimelineController.event.data.
  noofemployers}"
    required="true" label="Room" />

<h:outputText value="Applied posts" />
<p:inputText value="#
  {jobhubTimelineController.event.data.
  noofappliedposts}"
    required="true" label="Room" />
</h:panelGrid>
</h:panelGroup>


<f:facet name="footer">
<h:panelGroup layout="block" style="text-align:right;
  padding:2px; white-space:nowrap;">
  <p:commandButton value="Save"
    process="detailsJobhubDlg" update="@none"
    action="#{jobhubTimelineController.saveDetails}"
  oncomplete="if(!args.validationFailed)
    {PF('detailsJobhubWdgt').hide();}" />
  <p:commandButton type="button" value="Close"
    onclick="PF('detailsJobhubWdgt').hide()" />
</h:panelGroup>
  </f:facet>
</p:dialog>

<p:dialog id="deleteJobhubDlg" header="Jobhub Details"
  widgetVar="deleteJobhubWdgt" showEffect="clip"
    hideEffect="clip" dynamic="true">
  <h:panelGroup id="deleteJobhubInner" layout="block"
    style="margin:10px;">
```

```
        <h:outputText
          value="#{jobhubTimelineController.deleteMessage}"
          />
      </h:panelGroup>
       <f:facet name="footer">
      <h:panelGroup layout="block" style="text-align:right;
        padding:2px; white-space:nowrap;">
          <p:commandButton value="Delete"
            process="deleteJobhubDlg"
        update="@none"
          action="#{jobhubTimelineController.delete}"
              oncomplete="PF('deleteJobhubWdgt').hide()" />
          <p:commandButton type="button" value="Close"
            onclick="PF('deleteJobhubWdgt').hide()" />
      </h:panelGroup>
    </f:facet>
    </p:dialog>
```

2.  Create a managed bean with the TimeLine model with minimal configuration
    options as shown in the following code snippet:

```
privateTimelineModel model;
privateTimelineEvent event;
private long zoomMax;
private Date start;
private Date end;
privateTimeZonetimeZone = TimeZone.getTimeZone("Europe/Madrid");

@PostConstruct
protected void initialize() {
  zoomMax = 1000L * 60 * 60 * 24 * 30;
  model = new TimelineModel();
  Calendar cal = Calendar.getInstance();
  cal.set(2011, Calendar.MAY, 10, 0, 0, 0);
  Date start = cal.getTime();
  cal.set(2011, Calendar.MAY, 15, 0, 0, 0);
  Date end = cal.getTime();
  model.add(new TimelineEvent(new Jobhub("10000", "500",
"2000000"),start, end));
  //Add other TimeLine events
}
```

3. Create the following TimeLine CRUD operations in the server-side code using the Ajax event listener methods:

```
//CRUD Operations
public void onChange(TimelineModificationEvent e) {
  event = e.getTimelineEvent();
  model.update(event);
FacesMessagemsg = new FacesMessage(FacesMessage.SEVERITY_INFO,
  "The Post details of posts count " + getJobhubPosts()
    + " have been updated", null);
  FacesContext.getCurrentInstance().addMessage(null, msg);
}
public void onEdit(TimelineModificationEvent e) {
  event = e.getTimelineEvent();
}
public void onAdd(TimelineAddEvent e) {
  event = new TimelineEvent(new Jobhub(), e.getStartDate(),
      e.getEndDate(), true, e.getGroup());
  model.add(event);
}
public void onDelete(TimelineModificationEvent e) {
  event = e.getTimelineEvent();
}

public void delete() {
  TimelineUpdatertimelineUpdater = TimelineUpdater
      .getCurrentInstance(":adminForm:tabView:timeline");
  model.delete(event, timelineUpdater);

  FacesMessagemsg = new FacesMessage(FacesMessage.SEVERITY_INFO,
    "The posts details of posts count  " + getJobhubPosts()
          + " has been deleted", null);
  FacesContext.getCurrentInstance().addMessage(null, msg);
}
public void saveDetails() {
  TimelineUpdatertimelineUpdater = TimelineUpdater
    .getCurrentInstance(":adminForm:tabView:timeline");
  model.update(event, timelineUpdater);
  FacesMessagemsg = new FacesMessage(FacesMessage.SEVERITY_INFO,
    "The posts details of posts count " + getJobhubPosts()
          + " have been saved", null);
  FacesContext.getCurrentInstance().addMessage(null, msg);
}
```

4. Run the application and navigate to the admin's page with the URL `http://localhost:8080/jobhub/views/admin.xhtml` using the admin's role.

Now you are able to see the TimeLine component with multiple events as shown in the following screenshot:

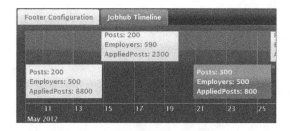

Double-click on any one of the events to make modifications or CRUD operations to the event as shown in the following screenshot:

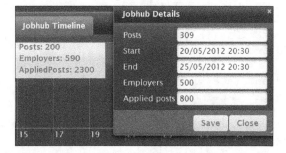

After the JobHub details are modified for a particular event, then the changes are reflected after submitting the changes as shown in the following screenshot:

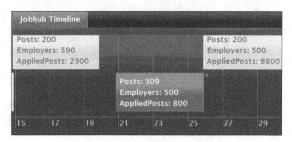

# Summary

In this chapter, you have been introduced to the time tracking and scheduling components that cover topics such as TimePicker for picking the exact time in a convenient way with more controls and the TimeLine component as an interactive visualization chart for event tracking/managing and internationalization support in time tracking components.

In the next chapter, we will take a detailed look at the data reporting components for extracting the large datasets in different file formats by developing the JobHub application and explaining image component features in image manipulation tasks.

# 6
# Extended Data Reporting and Image Components

Data iteration components named dataTable and dataList used to hold big datasets to display in the web page where the data is stored and retrieved from a database. However, it may not be possible to view the web page datasets when offline; also, tracking the data every time by logging into the site will be a time-consuming and difficult process. In this case, data reporting components' development in various formats is necessary and very helpful. Considering these requirements, the PrimeFaces Extensions library developed an exporter component targeting dataTable and dataList as reporting data components in most popular formats such as **PDF** and **Excel**.

In this chapter, we will cover the following topics:

- Introducing exporter components and explaining their features
- Understanding and implementing fully controlled custom exporters
- Working with Image components for image manipulation

## Introducing exporter components and its features

The PrimeFaces Core dataExporter component works very well on the plain dataTable components along with providing some custom features. But the PrimeFaces Extensions exporter component is introduced to work on all the major features of the dataTable component, provides full control of customization, and extends its features to dataList components.

The exporter component is used to extract and report the tabular form of data in different formats. This component is targeted to work with all major features of dataTable, subTable, and other data iteration components such as dataList as well. Currently, the supported file formats are PDF and Excel. Both `headerText` and `footerText` columns are supported along with the value holders.

Please refer to *Chapter 1, Introducing PrimeFaces Extensions*, to find out the additional JARs required for PDF and Excel formats.

 The exporter component works only with nonAjax command actions or calls. So you should remember to add the `ajax="false"` property for all the PrimeFaces command components.

The exporter component supports the following list of dataTable and dataList features:

- Multiple table export
- Grouping table export
- SubTable export
- Editable table export
- Customized format for dataTable export
- Expandable dataTable export
- Dynamic column export
- DataTable column alignments export
- DataList export

We will explain all the preceding exporter features with sample exporter code syntax. You can refer to the particular dataTable code syntax in JobHub's action part or the PrimeFaces Extensions showcase.

# Multiple table export

In many use cases, you may need to export multiple related tables at the same time instead of exporting each table separately. Considering this requirement, exporter component supported the multitable's export feature by configuring the comma-separated list of the dataTable server IDs or component IDs in the `target` attribute.

You can add space between the tables using the `datasetPadding` attribute.

There is no limit on the number of tables that can be exported at the same time. You can mention as many number of table IDs in the `target` attribute as you want.

Create the following XHTML code, which contains the exporter components to extract the **Account** table and the **Account details** table at the same time:

```
<p:panel header="Export data  PDF and Excel ">
    <p:commandLink id="pdf" ajax="false">
        <p:graphicImage value="/resources/images/pdf.png"/>
        <pe:exporter type="pdf" target="accountTable,accountDe
          tailsTable" fileName="AccountsAndDetails"
          datasetPadding="5"/>
    </p:commandLink>
    <p:spacer width="30"/>
    <p:commandLink id="xls" ajax="false">
        <p:graphicImage value="/resources/images/excel.png"/>
        <pe:exporter type="xlsx" target="accountTable,accountDetailsT
          able" fileName="AccountsAndDetails" datasetPadding="5"/>
    </p:commandLink>
</p:panel>
```

You have to remember to place the comma separated list of dataTable components IDs for the multiTable export.

# Grouping table export

Grouping tables (tables that contain multiple columns divided as related sets or chunks) formed with the combination of header and footer facets using the different `rowSpans` and `colSpans` columns can be exported using the exporter component. There are no additional configurations or settings required to use this feature.

Grouping tables should contain columns with the `rowSpan` and `colSpan` properties only under the child columnGroup and row tags.

# SubTable export

SubTable is another variation of the dataTable component, or a helper component of the dataTable component for grouping related datasets in the parent datasets. You can export the SubTable component by changing the `subtable` attribute to `true`.

Create the following XHTML code, which contains the exporter component to extract the sales subtable component. Here you need to make sure that the subtable attribute is set to true.

```
<p:panel header="Export data to PDF and Excel ">
    <p:commandLink id="pdf" ajax="false">
        <p:graphicImage value="/resources/images/pdf.png"/>
        <pe:exporter type="pdf" target="salesSubTable"
          fileName="salesStatistics" subTable="true"/>
    </p:commandLink>
    <p:spacer width="30"/>
    <p:commandLink id="xls" ajax="false">
        <p:graphicImage value="/resources/images/excel.png"/>
        <pe:exporter type="xlsx" target="salesSubTable"
           fileName="salesStatistics" subTable="true"  />
    </p:commandLink>
</p:panel>
```

# Editable table export

The dataTable's rowEditing and cellEditing features allow editing the dataTable rows' and cells' content respectively at one instance. Both input and select components from JavaSever Faces and PrimeFaces libraries are supported as content while exporting. There are no additional settings required to support this feature in export.

# Customized format for dataTable export

The customized format feature allows exporting the table with customized skinning for header, footer, and cell contents with different fonts and background colors. You can add titles to your exported files with the help of the tableTitle attribute.

The attributes supported with this feature are listed in a tabular format as follows:

| Custom format options | Description |
|---|---|
| facetBackground | This is the hexadecimal colors for header and footer facets. |
| facetFontSize | This is the header and footer facet font size. |
| facetFontColor | This is the hexadecimal color codes for header and footer font colors. |
| facetFontStyle | This is the header and footer font styles. The possible values are normal, italics, and bold. The default value is bold. |

| Custom format options | Description |
|---|---|
| cellFontSize | This is the cell content's font size. |
| cellFontColor | This is the hexadecimal color codes for cell content.. |
| cellFontStyle | This defines the cell content's font styles. The possible values are normal, italics, and bold. The default value is normal. |
| fontName | This defines the font name or font style to be used. |
| orientation | This defines the PDF format. The possible values are Portrait and Landscape. The default value is Portrait. |

You can also use preProcessor and postProcessor to customize the reported file such as adding logos and disclaimers.. Conversely, the pageOnly and selectionOnly properties allow data that can be exported with the current page data and the current selection data respectively.

The following XHTML code creates an exporter component with all the possible custom format options:

```
<p:panel header="Export PDF and Excel data">
    <p:commandLink id="pdf" ajax="false">
        <p:graphicImage value="/resources/images/pdf.png"/>
        <pe:exporter type="pdf" target="investmentsTable"
          fileName="InvestmentsTable" tableTitle="Investements
          Analysis" orientation="Landscape"
          facetBackground="#FF00FF" facetFontSize="12"
          facetFontColor="#ff00ff" facetFontStyle="BOLD"
          cellFontColor="#00fff0" cellFontSize="10"
          cellFontStyle="NORMAL"/>
    </p:commandLink>
    <p:spacer height="30"/>
    <p:commandLink id="xlsx" ajax="false">
        <p:graphicImage value="/resources/images/excel.png"/>
        <pe:exporter type="xlsx" target="investmentsTable"
          fileName="InvestmentsTable" tableTitle="Investements
          Analysis"
          facetBackground="#DD017" facetFontSize="12"
          facetFontColor="#ff00ff" facetFontStyle="BOLD"
          fontName="Courier New" cellFontColor="#00ff00"
          cellFontSize="10" cellFontStyle="NORMAL"/>
    </p:commandLink>
</p:panel>
```

Both the PDF and Excel export formats are affected by the customized format options with rich skinning and styles.

# Expandable table export

In order to display the additional information of each data record, dataTable will use the rowExpansion tag that contains dataTable/dataList containers to show the data. There are no additional settings required to use this feature.

# Dynamic column export

DataTable columns can be defined dynamically using the p:columns tag instead of using the regular p:column component. You can also add or remove the columns programmatically because the columns are created on demand. You don't require any special settings or configurations to export dynamic columns.

# DataTable column alignments

The DataTable column content is aligned with different alignment styles such as left, center, and right values depending on the content type. In any application, numeric data is aligned to the right and text data is aligned to the left or center. The reported data won't contain the web page's dataTable alignments by default, but the exporter component supports the column alignments by mentioning the alignments with the style attribute.

The default alignment for the header or footer facets is center, whereas, the default alignment for cell content is left.

The alignment values for float property affect both the web page and reported data. Conversely, the alignment values without the float property affect only the reported data.

```
< h:outputText value="left aligned content" style="float:left" >
<h:outputText value="right aligned content" style="float:right" >
< h:outputText value="center aligned content" style="center" >
```

 To work with custom column alignments, just use the style attributes that hold either the left, center, or right values.

# DataList export

DataList is used to represent the collection of data in a list-formatted layout with various display types. The children of dataList can be either column or plain output value holders. The exporter also supports the dataList component along with the dataTable component. You just need to refer its component ID instead of the dataTable component ID.

# JobHub in action

Let us see how the exporter features named **expandable table export** and **customized format table export** implemented for the list of registered companies display under the employer's list screen, as follows:

1. Create the following XHTML code to implement the export expandable feature for the employer's additional details:

```
<p:panel header="Export data  to PDF and Excel ">
    <p:commandLink id="pdf" ajax="false">
        <p:graphicImage value="/resources/images/exporticons/pdf.
          png" />
        <f:setPropertyActionListener value="false"
          target="#{exporterController.customExporter}" />
        <pe:exporter type="pdf" target="employerList"
          fileName="Employer Details" facetBackground="#008000"
          facetFontSize="15" facetFontColor="#FFFFFF"
          facetFontStyle="BOLD" cellFontColor="#0000FF"
          cellFontSize="12"
          cellFontStyle="NORMAL" fontName="Courier New" />
    </p:commandLink>
    <p:spacer width="20" />
    <p:commandLink id="xls" ajax="false">
        <p:graphicImage value="/resources/images/exporticons/excel.
          png" />
        <f:setPropertyActionListener value="false"
          target="#{exporterController.customExporter}" />
        <pe:exporter type="xlsx" target="employerList"
          fileName="Employer Details" facetBackground="#F88017"
          facetFontSize="10" facetFontColor="#0000ff"
          facetFontStyle="BOLD"  fontName="Courier New"
          cellFontColor="#00ff00"
          cellFontSize="8" cellFontStyle="NORMAL"/>
    </p:commandLink>
</p:panel>
```

We enabled the `customExporter` flag to implement the custom exporter feature, which should not affect other exporter use cases in the JobHub application.

2. Run the application and navigate to the employer's list screen with the `http://localhost:8080/jobhub/views/employerslist.xhtml` URL using the employer's role.

Clicking on the PDF export button results in the row expandable table with customized format of data reports as shown in the following screenshot:

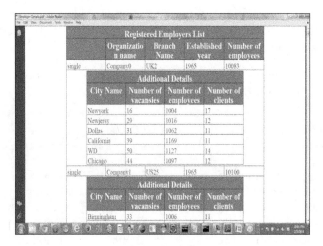

Clicking on the Excel button retrieves the datasets in the Excel format as shown in the following screenshot:

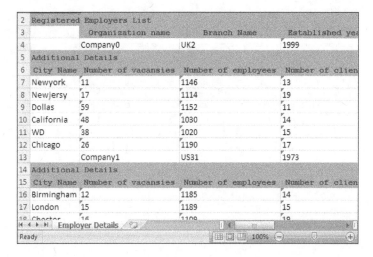

As you can see from the preceding screenshots, there is no limit to creating custom formatted dataTables in the PDF and Excel data reports.

# Understanding and implementing fully controlled custom exporter

The custom exporter provides full control to the developer for making the changes according to his requirements and design. You can implement the custom requirements in both `PDFExporter` and `ExcelExporter` implementations.

You have to use the **Service Loader** concept throughout the application to implement the custom exporter feature.

Proceed with the following steps to implement the custom exporter feature:

1. Create the `META-INF` folder under the classpath resources folder and create the services folder under the `META-INF` folder by navigating to **Resources | META-INF | Services**.

2. Create the `ExporterFactory` file with the full absolute path as `org.primefaces.extensions.component.exporter.ExporterFactory`.

3. Add the implementation class of ExporterFactory in the web project.

   For example, the JobHub application provided CustomExporterFactory as an implementation of ExporterFactory.

   In the following code, you will call either default or custom file formats based on the Boolean flag property configured with the export component:

```java
public class CustomExporterFactory implements ExporterFactory {
    static public enum ExporterType {
        PDF,
        XLSX
    }
    public Exporter getExporterForType(String type) {
        Exporter exporter = null;
        FacesContext context = FacesContext.getCurrentInstance();
        ExporterController bean = (ExporterController)
    context.getApplication().evaluateExpressionGet(context,
    "#{exporterController}", ExporterController.class);
        Boolean    customExport=bean.getCustomExporter();
        try {
            ExporterType exporterType =
                ExporterType.valueOf(type.toUpperCase());
            switch (exporterType) {
```

```
                    case PDF:
                        if(customExport) {
                        exporter = new PDFCustomExporter();
                        }
                        else {
                        exporter = new PDFExporter();
                        }
                        break;
                    case XLSX:
                        if(customExport) {
                            exporter = new
                            ExcelCustomExporter();
                        }
                        else {

                            exporter = new ExcelExporter();
                        }
                        break;
                    default: {
                        if(customExport) {
                            exporter = new PDFCustomExporter();
                        }
                        else {
                            exporter = new PDFExporter();
                        }
                        break;
                    }
                }
            } catch (IllegalArgumentException e) {
                throw new FacesException(e);
            }
            return exporter;
        }
    }
```

4. Copy the absolute path of the ExporterFactory implementation as the content in the file that is placed under the `services` folder.

   For example, the JobHub application configured the ExporterFactory implementation in the file that resides under the `services` folder. The package name is as follows:

   `com.packt.pfextensions.util.CustomExporterFactory`

5. Copy the exporter implementations such as PDFExporter and ExcelExporter from the PrimeFaces Extensions code base into your project and make changes as per your requirements.

These customized exporter implementations are called instead of calling the default exporter implementations in the ExporterFactory implementation.

For example, the JobHub application added index columns to the exporter implementations.

# JobHub in action

Let us implement the following custom exporter feature of the exporter component by adding the index columns to the exporter implementations as a JobHub application requirement:

1. Create the following XHTML page with custom exporter features of the exporter component on the list of all job posts table:

```
<p:panel header="Export data to PDF and Excel">
    <p:commandLink id="pdf" ajax="false">
<p:graphicImage value="/resources/images/exporticons/pdf.png" />
    <f:setPropertyActionListener value="true"
      target="#{exporterController.customExporter}" />
     <pe:exporter type="pdf" target="posts" fileName="posts" />
    </p:commandLink>
    <p:spacer width="20" />
    <p:commandLink id="xls" ajax="false">
  <p:graphicImage value="/resources/images/exporticons/excel.png"
  />
    <f:setPropertyActionListener value="true"
      target="#{exporterController.customExporter}" />
     <pe:exporter type="xlsx" target="posts" fileName="posts" />
    </p:commandLink>
</p:panel>
```

2. Run the application and navigate to the jobsList page with the http://localhost:8080/jobhub/views/jobsList.xhtml URL using the JobSeeker's role.

3. Click on the PDF icon to extract the list of posts and it opens the PDF, as shown in the following screenshot:

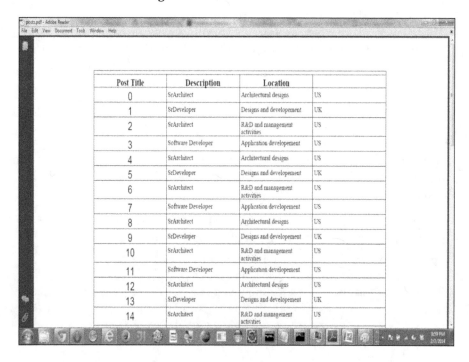

4. Click on the Excel icon to extract the list of jobs and it opens Excel as shown in the following screenshot:

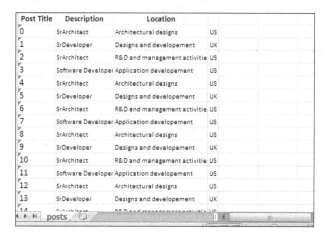

Now you are able to see the index column in both PDF and Excel formats using the custom exporter feature.

# Working with image components for image manipulation

The PrimeFaces Extensions library provided two image widget components for image manipulations. The **ImageAreaSelect** and **ImageRotateAndResize** widget components are used to select a rectangular area of the image and rotate and resize the images with the support of widget functions and events.

## Exploring the ImageAreaSelect widget

The ImageAreaSelect widget is used for selecting a rectangular area of the image to support image cropping functionalities in the web user interface.

This component supports customizations with the use of the following attributes:

| Property | Description |
| --- | --- |
| authHide | This defines whether the selection area needs to disappear when the selection ends or not. The default value is `false`. |
| aspectRatio | This defines the aspect ratio in the `width:height` string form. |
| Handles | This defines the resized handle's position and existence. The possible values are `corners`, `true` (selection area), and `false`. |
| Movable | This defines whether the selection area is movable or not. The default value is `false`. |
| Persistent | This defines whether to store the selection area on blur action or not. The default value is `false`. |
| Resizable | This defines whether the selection area needs to be resizable or not. The default value is `true`. |
| keyboardSupport | This defines whether to enable/disable keyboard support. The default value is `false`. |

The following XHTML code contains the ImageAreaSelect component with configurable custom options:

```
<pe:imageAreaSelect id="areaSelect" for="imageID"
    autoHide="true" aspectratio="4:3" handles="false"
    movable="false"
    persistent="false" resizable="false" keyboardSupport="true">
        <p:ajax event="selectEnd" listener="#{imageAreaSelectContr
            oller.selectEndListener}"/>
</pe:imageAreaSelect>
```

Now you have applied the ImageAreaSelect component on any image component with customized options.

# Understanding the ImageRotateAndResize widget

The ImageRotateAndResize widget is used to resize or rotate images and catch the images on the server side by receiving the events. Behind the scenes, this component uses HTML5 Canvas to support or be compatible with all the browsers. Older IE browsers are compatible with the use of Matrix Filter.

This component supports the following widget functions:

- **rotateLeft** (degree): This rotates the image to the left
- **rotateRight** (degree): This rotates the image to the right
- **resize** (width, height): This resizes the image to the given width and height
- **scale** (scaleFactor): This scales the image with the given factor
- **restoreDefaults()**: This restores the default image

You can use either Ajax behavior or the pe:javascript components to catch the rotate and resize events.

The following XHTML code creates the imageRotateAndResize component on any image component with rotate and resize events:

```
<h:graphicImage id="galleryimage" value="/resources/images/
galleryimage.png" />
<pe:imageRotateAndResize id="rotateAndResize" for="galleryimage" widge
    tVar="rotateAndResizeWidget">
    <p:ajax event="rotate" listener="#{imageRotateAndResizeController.
        rotateListener}"/>
    <pe:javascript event="resize" execute="alert('resize event
        fired')"/>
</pe:imageRotateAndResize>
<p:commandButton icon="ui-icon-arrowreturnthick-1-w" value="Rotate
    Left" onclick="PF('rotateAndResizeWidget').rotateLeft(90);return
    false;"/>
<p:commandButton icon="ui-icon-arrowreturnthick-1-e" value="Rotate
    Right" onclick="PF('rotateAndResizeWidget').rotateRight(180);return
    false;"/>
```

```
<p:commandButton icon="ui-icon-zoomin" value="Scale +"
        onclick="PF('rotateAndResizeWidget').scale(1.5);return
        false;"/>
<p:commandButton icon="ui-icon-zoomout" value="Scale -"
        onclick="PF('rotateAndResizeWidget').scale(0.5);return
        false;"/>
```

# Summary

In this chapter, you were introduced to the extended data reporting component and image components to explain exporting data iterative components that are available with many features, and custom exporter implementation and image components to work on the image manipulations. At the end of this chapter, you learned all the possible features of the export component and how to apply them in the PrimeFaces application.

In the next chapter, we will take a detailed look into the common utility components, functions, and plugins to ease frequent web development tasks and their role in the JSF application development.

# 7
# Common Utility Solutions, Error Handling, and Plugins

The PrimeFaces Extensions team introduced a few useful common utility components and functions that are used to solve the frequently recurring issues encountered in our daily JSF- or PrimeFaces-based development. These components can also be used to make development easier. On the other hand, the new Maven plugin is developed for web resource optimization by compressing, merging JS/CSS files, and optimizing image loading using the concept of data URIs.

In this chapter, we will cover the following topics:

- Common utility components, functions, and their features
- The Ajax error handling component and its usage
- The Maven resource optimizer plugin and its features

## Common utility components, functions, and their features

Common utility components are used to solve problems occurring in daily development and make development easier during the development of JSF or the PrimeFaces application. Among these components, JavaScript client behaviors, which is used to catch the events, converters to work with JSON and locale conversions, and common functions and utilities for regular development activities, will be considered as a part of the common utility components.

# Exploring the ClientBehaviour components

Client behaviors are used to catch events with JavaScript without making any Ajax request. When the functionality requires only the client-side JavaScript execution without any required server interaction, then the `pe:javascript` component is really useful.

 If you use this client behavior for the functionalities that depend on Ajax calls, then it will destroy the main functionality. So, you have to use this component only for the particular components and events where it is required.

The `pe:javascript` tag is defined with three attributes: **event** for the name of the event, **execute** for JavaScript functions to be executed, and **disabled** for defining whether to enable/disable the JavaScript behavior.

Attach the JavaScript client behavior (using the event and execute attributes) to any JSF or PrimeFaces component using the following code:

```
<pe:javascript event="eventname" execute="alert('JS function
    executed')"/>
```

# Understanding commonly used converter components

Converters are introduced in the Extensions library for converting the JSON string representation and locale strings into the backing bean properties. You can use these components by attaching them to the JSF or PF components instead of writing your own custom converters every time in the web project.

## JSON to bean property conversions using JsonConverter

JsonConverter can be used to convert the JSON representation to backing bean properties and vice versa. In real time, the major use cases of JsonConverter are used to work with the remoteCommand and viewParam components. Please refer to *Chapter 2, Enhanced Form and Editor Components*, to get more details about the remoteCommand component usage.

## Using JsonConverter with remoteCommand

You can use JsonConverter with the combination of the remoteCommand and assignableParam components. The remoteCommand component has assignableParam components as its children. They accept plain JavaScript parameters and JSON string representation. To convert the JSON string representation to a backing bean property, the `pe:convertJson` component will be very helpful. Only the **type** attribute is used to specify any primitive, generic, or non-generic datatypes to the JSON representation conversion.

In the following sample code, `pe:convertJson` is attached to the `assignableParam` tag. The following XHTML code is used to send the sales details from the client-side JSON representation to the server-side bean with the help of the `pe:convertJson` component:

```
<pe:remoteCommand id="applySalesCommand" name="applySales" process="@
  this"
    actionListener="#{remoteCommandController.parametersAssigned}">
    <pe:assignableParam name="branch"
      assignTo="#{remoteCommandController.branch}"/>
    <pe:assignableParam name="circle" assignTo="#{remoteCommandContro
      ller.sales}">
        <pe:convertJson />
    </pe:assignableParam>
</pe:remoteCommand>
<script type="text/javascript">
    sales = {
        revenue: $50,
        gain: $20,
        profit: 30%
    };
</script>
<p:commandButton value="Apply Data" type="button"
  onclick="applySales'UK',JSON.stringif(sales))" />
```

## Using JsonConverter with ViewParams

JsonConverter can also be used to convert URL parameters to a backing bean property. You can provide this functionality by just attaching `pe:convertJson` to the `f:viewParam` tag. Only the type attribute supports primitive, generic, or non-generic datatypes of value objects.

The ViewParams use case can be achieved in a two-step process as follows:

1.  Use `RequestParameterBuilder` to build URL parameters to JSON representation.

2.  Then apply `pe:convertJson` for converting the JSON string representation to a bean property.

Create the following XHTML code by attaching various datatypes (date and list used here) of the `convertJson` components to the `viewParam` tags:

```
<!-- f:metadata on this page -->
<f:metadata>
    <f:viewParam name="d" value="#{jsonController.d}">
        <pe:convertJson type="java.util.Date"/>
    </f:viewParam>
    <f:viewParam name="list" value="#{jsonController.list}">
        <pe:convertJson type="#{jsonController.typeGenericList}"/>
    </f:viewParam>
</f:metadata>
<p:inputText id="inputUrl"
  value="#{jsonController.generatedUrl}"/>
<p:commandButton value="Open Link" type="button"
                 onclick="openLinkPopup()"/>
<h:outputScript id="jsonConverterJS" target="body">
    function openLinkInPopup() {
        var inputValue = $('#inputUrl').val();
        if (inputValue !== null) {
            window.open(inputValue, 'JsonConverter with URL
            parameters', 'width=auto,height=auto,resizable=yes,scroll
            bars=yes');
        }
    }
</h:ou tputScript>
```

Create the JSON string representation of the URL with the required parameters using the `RequestParameterBuilder` class. Here, we created the following JSON representation with the date and list parameters:

```
private String generatedUrl;
    @PostConstruct
    protected void initialize() {
        // creates a builder instance with current request URL
        RequestParameterBuilder rpBuilder = new
    RequestParameterBuilder(true);
```

```
Collection<Integer> list = new ArrayList<Integer>();
               list.add("Hello");
               list.add("PFExt");
               list.add("reader");
       try {
   rpBuilder.paramJson("d", new Date());
           rpBuilder.paramJson("list", list, getTypeGenericList());

   } catch (UnsupportedEncodingException e) {
           // handle encoding issues
       }
       // build URL
       generatedUrl = rpBuilder.build();
   public String getTypeGenericList() {
       return "java.util.Collection<java.lang.String>";
   }
}
```

# Locale converter

The locale converter can be used to convert the locale string to a locale object type and vice versa (that is, convert the locale string type to the `java.util.Locale` object type). This converter is quite useful when the locale string type that is entered from the UI needs to be converted to a locale object in the server side and vice versa. The most common use case is applying the locale converter component on the selected language option to change the locale dynamically.

Create the following XHTML code by attaching the locale converter to the locale input component:

```
<p:inputText id="enteredLocale" value="#{localeController.
enteredLocale}" required="true">
    <pe:convertLocale/>
</p:inputText>
```

# Functions and utilities

A few common functions and utility components are added to solve daily occurring problems and also to create developer-friendly helper components.

# Introducing common functions

Some common **EL** (**Expression Language**) functions are introduced for **escaping** or **unescaping** the HTML and XML contents and also for encoding the URL content. These functions optimize the application performance over the escaped/unescaped bean content of `h:outputText`. In JSF, the inline code always improves the application performance up to some level. Using these common functions, you can escape the content just by adding it as an inline code without using the outputText component.

The following unescaped function is used to unesacape the HTML 4 content:

```
Output : #{pe:unescapedHTML4(bean.value)}
```

The managed bean contains the following HTML-specific text inside value property:

```
String value="<b>Extensions</b>";
```

The unescaped function generates the following output:

Output: **Extensions**.

The following table lists out all the functions with their descriptions:

| Function name | Function description |
|---|---|
| escapeHtml4 or unescapeHtml4 | This escapes or unescapes HTML 4 entities |
| escapeHtml3 or unescapeHtml3 | This escapes or unescapes HTML 3 entities |
| escapeXml or unescapeXml | This escapes or unescapes XML entities |
| encodeURL | This encodes the URL |

# Utilities to ease the web development tasks

To solve the commonly occurring issues in the JSF development, the Extensions library introduced a few utility components or functions.

## Understanding the importConstants utility

In EL 2.2 or older versions, you can't access any constants or static fields/methods in an EL expression. Instead of writing or creating beans with the setters and getters for each constant class, you can add the utilities tag that imports all the constants in a file.

 The constants can be accessed via the default name of the class or via the custom `var` attribute name.

The following XHTML code represents the usage of `importConstants` to import constant values:

```
<pe:importConstants className="org.primefaces.extensions.util.
Constants" var="PFEConstants" />
Library Name:
<h:outputText value="#{PFEConstants.LIBRARY}" />
```

## Understanding the importEnum utility

You can also import the enum constants in your web page by adding the enum utility tag at the top of the page. All the enum values of the class can be accessed through the **"ALL_VALUES"** suffix or using a custom suffix via the `allSuffix` attribute as follows:

```
<pe:importEnum type="javax.faces.application.ProjectStage"
var="JsfProjectStages" allSuffix="ALL_ENUM" />
Current stage:
Development: #{JsfProjectStages.Development}
All stages:
<ui:repeat var="current" value="#{JsfProjectStages.ALL_ENUM}">
  <h:outputText value="#{current}" />
</ui:repeat>
```

The following `enum` class is defined with all the project stages:

```
public enum ProjectStage {
    Development,
    UnitTest,
    SystemTest,
    UserAcceptanceTest,
    Production;
}
```

## Understanding the escapeSelector utility

jQuery normally understands the colon (:) symbol as CSS pseudo class. You have to escape the colon character in order get the correct client path in JSF. You can use the `escapeSelector` function to escape the colon characters in the JSF client ID path.

The following sample syntax shows how applying `escapeSelector` on the client ID path (which resides in the form tag as it was formed by the dataTable component) results in backslashes (\\) before the colon symbol:

Output: #{pe:escapeSelector('form:table')}

It generates the output client path as follows:

Output: `form\\:table`

## Choosing options using the switch component

Many times you may need to display outputs or components depending on an input value provided. You can achieve this functionality in the standard JSF with the help of the `ui:fragment` tag on each possible option with conditional rendering. This task can be easier with the `switch` tag.

As an example, the following `switch` tag enables menu selection based on the user input value:

```
<pe:switch id="switch" value="#{switchController.input}">
    <pe:defaultCase>
        Default: Icecreams
    </pe:defaultCase>
    <pe:case value="case1">
        Menu1: <p:commandButton id="icecreams" ajax="false"
                value="Go to icecreams option" />
    </pe:case>
    <pe:case value="case2">
        Menu2: <p:commandButton id="juice"
                value="Go to juice option"  />
    </pe:case>
    <pe:case value="#{null}">
        No option selected
    </pe:case>
</pe:switch>
```

# JobHub in action

Let us apply the ClientBehaviours and JsonConverter component features in our JobHub applications.

## Applying the ClientBehaviour component

First, we will navigate to the companiesList screen, where it displays the images with animated opacity and displays **Top** when it reaches the end of the scroll.

Here, we used the `pe:javascript` ClientBehaviour component to execute the custom JavaScript logic and attach the custom CSS script.

You have to proceed with the following step-by-step procedure to work with the ClientBehaviour component:

1. Create the following XHTML code that contains multiple ClientBehaviour components named `pe:javascript` attached to a different Waypoint component.

   First, the `pe:javascript` component is used to execute the logic for loading the images with opacity.

   ```
   <pe:waypoint id="waypoint" offset="'100%'">
   <pe:javascript event="reached" execute="handleWaypoint(ext);" />
   </pe:waypoint>
   ```

   Conversely, the second `pe:javascript` component is used to toggle the style class of the **Top** button.

   ```
   <pe:waypoint id="waypoint1" offset="'-100%'">
   <pe:javascript event="reached"
   execute="$('.ui-button').toggleClass('hidden');" />
   </pe:waypoint>
   ```

2. Run the application and navigate to the JobSeeker's `jobsList` screen. Now, you click on the companies' link, which navigates to the companies' list page with the `http://localhost:8080/jobhub/views/companiesList.xhtml` URL.

   If you scroll down the page, then you will see the images loaded with animation and the **TOP** button, which is shown in the following screenshot, appears when the scroller reaches the end:

Clicking on the **TOP** button scrolls the web page to the top of the screen.

# The JsonConverter component

Let us navigate to the employer's employersList page where you can find the CMMI level of the companies' standard section. Clicking on any one of the CMMI level buttons populates the company's standards.

Here, we used the pe:convertJson component in combination with the pe:remoteCommand component to covert the JSON string to a bean property.

You have to proceed with the following step-by-step procedure to work with the JsonConverter component:

1. Create the following XHTML code that contains the pe:convertJson component attached to the assignableParam child tag of the remoteCommand component:

```
<pe:remoteCommand id="applyDataCommand" name="applyData"
  process="@this" update="focus result standards">
  <pe:assignableParam name="focus"
    assignTo="#{employerDetailsController.focus}" />
  <pe:assignableParam name="result"
    assignTo="#{employerDetailsController.result}"/>
  <pe:assignableParam name="standards"
    assignTo="#{employerDetailsController.standards}">
    <pe:convertJson />
  </pe:assignableParam>
</pe:remoteCommand>
<script type="text/javascript">
  cmmi3 = {
     years : 5,
     employees : "2k",
     revenue : "10mil"
    };
  cmmi5 = {
     years : 10,
     employees : "5k",
     revenue : "90mil",
    };
</script>
<p:commandButton value="CMMI3" type="button"
  onclick="applyData('Continuous Process Improvement',
  'Highest Quality', JSON.stringify(cmmi3))" />
<p:commandButton value="CMMI5" type="button"
  onclick="applyData('Process Standardization', 'Medium
  Quality ', JSON.stringify(cmmi5))" />
```

2. Run the application and navigate to the employer's employersList screen with the `http://localhost:8080/jobhub/views/employerslist.xhtml` URL using employer's role.

   If you click on either the **CMMI3** or **CMMI5** buttons, then you can see the company's standards populated, as shown in the following screenshot:

Here, we grouped the company's standards in the JSON string representation and used JsonConverter to convert the JSON representation to the standards property of the employerDetailsController bean.

# The Ajax error handling component and its usage

If a partial Ajax throws an error, PrimeFaces web applications won't respond to the error. The developer won't be aware where the root cause for this issue is and how to overcome the issue to proceed further. The Ajax errors occur frequently when the action listener throws an exception during the DB save operation or when the session expires the use cases. After the session expires, the user action has no effect on the web page.

To overcome these use cases, the Extensions library introduced `pe:ajaxErrorHandler` to display the messages in case of an Ajax error detection. You can customize the messages based on the type of error as well.

This component supports both the simple and extended modes. You can activate the extended mode by setting `exception-handler-factory` in the `faces-config.xml` file. The extended mode resolves the session expired issues when you set `STATE-SAVING_METHOD=server` and `PARTIAL_STATE_SAVING=false`.

Configure `exception-handler-factor` in your `faces-config.xml` file for activating the extended mode as follows:

```
<factory>
  <exception-handler-factory>org.primefaces.extensions.component.
    ajaxerrorhandler.AjaxExceptionHandlerFactory
  </exception-handler-factory>
</factory>
```

Now, you are going to learn the major features of AjaxErrorHandler.

# Customized messages

The content of the messages is customized with the help of the title, body, and button definition attributes. You can also localize the message content of these attributes.

The AjaxErrorHandler component supports the following list of template variables in a tabular format:

| Variable | Description |
| --- | --- |
| {error-name} | This is the full name of the exception/error |
| {error-message} | This is the message of the exception/error |
| {error-stacktrace} | This is the stack trace of the exception/error, but it only works for the extended mode |
| {error-hostname} | This is the hostname of the server where an exception is caught, but it only works for the extended mode |

The default usage of AjaxErrorHandler is as follows:

```
<pe:ajaxErrorHandler title="{error-name}" body="{error-message}"
button="Reload" />
```

> Both title and body text messages are also customized with facets. However, these facets will work only on the extended mode.

The following XHTML code explains how to customize error messages using different variables along with the title and head facets:

```
<pe:ajaxErrorHandler type="java.lang.IllegalStateException"
button="Reload the page!!">
    <f:facet name="title">
        Error <span style="color: red;">{error-name}</span>
    </f:facet>
```

```
<f:facet name="body">
    <h:form>
        <p:tabView >
            <p:tab title="Message">
                <h:panelGrid columns="2">
                    <h:outputLabel value="Error message:" />
                    <h:outputText value="{error-message}" />
                    <h:outputLabel value="Server name:" />
                    <h:outputText value="{error-hostname}"/>
                </h:panelGrid>
            </p:tab>
            <p:tab title="Detail">
                        {error-stacktrace}
            </p:tab>
        </p:tabView>
    </h:form>
</f:facet>
</pe:ajaxErrorHandler>
```

Click on the `Custom handler` button, which throws an illegal state exception in the server side, as shown in the following code:

```
<p:commandButton action="#{ajaxErrorHandlerController.
    actionFiredException}" value="Custom handler" />
public String actionFiredException() {
        Throwable t = new IllegalStateException("This is an illegal
            state exception!");
        throw new FacesException(t);
    }
```

Instead of applying the default variables, you can also apply the custom descriptions for the message's content. The type attribute specifies the behavior of the component.

For example, the description of `ViewExpiredException` can be used as `"Due to inactivity the page needs to be RELOADED"`, as shown in the following code:

```
<pe:ajaxErrorHandler type="javax.faces.application.
        ViewExpiredException" button="Reload Page"
        buttonOnclick="document.location.href=document.location.href;"
        body="Due to inactivity the page needs to be RELOADED"
        title="Page is expired"/>
```

# Custom styles and layout definition

You can also overwrite default CSS classes with custom styles for the overlay masking and button colors.

The following custom style classes are used to overwrite the built-in style classes:

```
<!-- Custom CSS styles -->
<style type="text/css">
    /*Blue background for mask*/
    #ajaxErrorHandlerDialog\:modal {
        background: darkblue;
    }
    /*button colors*/
    #ajaxErrorHandlerDialog button * {
        color: red;
        background:none;
    }
    #ajaxErrorHandlerDialog button {
        border-width: 5px;
        background: lightred;
    }
</style>
```

You can also provide the custom layout definition by inserting the various styles and JSF or PrimeFaces components. However, you need to make sure that any component doesn't contain any `h:form` or Ajax behavior events.

You can also define the `ui-dialog-titlebar` and `ui-dialog-content` styleClasses for enabling and disabling the handle-mouse icon for draggable features.

# JobHub in action

Let us try to add the `pe:ajaxErrorHandler` component in our JobHub application to track Ajax errors occurring due to page inactivity using the following steps:

1. Create the following XHTML code that contains `pe:ajaxErrorHandler` to notify the view expired message:

```
<pe:ajaxErrorHandler
    type="javax.faces.application.ViewExpiredException"
    button="Reload"
    buttonOnclick="document.location.href=document.location.href;"
    body="Due to inactivity on page please push RELOAD to
    continue." title="Page expired ..." />
```

2. Run the application and navigate to any one of the pages in the JobHub application. To demonstrate the use case, let us navigate to the JobSeeker's `jobsList` page with the `http://localhost:8080/jobhub/views/jobsList.xhtml` URL using the JobSeeker's role.

After being idle for some time, AjaxErrorHandler throws a view expired exception in the JobHub application as follows:

You can reload the page by clicking on the **Reload** button to activate the web page again.

# The Maven resource optimizer plugin and its features

The PrimeFaces Extensions team provided a Maven resource plugin for optimizing resources. The resources can be optimized by compressing and merging the JS/CSS files and optimizing the loading of images using data URIs.

The Maven plugin integrates **Google compiler closure** and **YUI compressor** by taking advantage of both the plugins. The Google compiler closure provides better compression results for JavaScript files compared to the YUI compressor. However, the Google compiler can't be used for CSS files' compression; you have to use YUI compressor for it. The resource optimization provided by this plugin was better than the **YUI-Compression** plugin.

Each JavaScript file was better compressed in the simple mode itself, but in the advanced mode, the difference was dramatic. However, you need to be careful when using the advanced mode because unused functions were removed entirely.

## Setting up and configuring the plugin

The Maven plugin for resource optimization is available in the Maven repository. You just need to configure the following Maven dependency in your `pom.xml` file:

```
<plugin>
    <groupId>org.primefaces.extensions</groupId>
    <artifactId>resources-optimizer-maven-plugin</artifactId>
```

```
      <version>1.0.0</version>
       <executions>
         <execution>
           <id>optimize</id>
           <goals>
             <goal>optimize</goal>
           </goals>
         </execution>
       </executions>
       <configuration>
       <inputDir>${project.build.directory}/your_resource_directory</
  inputDir>
       </configuration>
  </plugin>
```

# Optimized image loading using the Data URIs' concept

The optimized loading of images can be done with the help of the Data URIs' concept. Data URIs allow any file to be embedded in line with the CSS. This mechanism allows separate image files to be fetched in a single HTTP request instead of consuming multiple HTTP requests. Thus, by decreasing the number of HTTP requests, you can improve page performance.

Data URIs are supported in all modern browsers but, for IE8, data URIs must be smaller than 32 KB.

## How the conversion works?

The Maven plugin first reads the content of CSS files by searching the **#{resource[...]}** tokens as follows:

```
.ui-icon-logo {
    background-image: url("#{resource['images/logo.gif']}")
  !important;
}
```

Next, the image resources for each background image are localized by referring the resources in WAR and JAR projects. The resources for WAR and JAR files are located in directories `${project.basedir}/src/main/webapp/resources` and `${project.basedir}/src/main/resources/META-INF/resources`, respectively. If the resources are not found in the directories or if the data URL size is more than 32 KB, then the images can't be transformed.

Now, after transformation into the `base64` code, the Data URIs are as follows:

```
.ui-icon-logo {
    background-image:
  url("data:image/gif;base64,iVBORw0KGgoAAAANSUhEUgA ...
    ASUVORK5CYII=") !important;
}
```

> By default, all the comments in the JS and CSS files are removed. Sometimes, you may need to preserve the comments that may exist in the form of copyright and license terms of use.
>
> To preserve comments in the CSS files, you may need to add an exclamation mark (!) before opening the /* sign, as follows:
>
> /*! some copyright information here */
>
> On the other hand, you can preserve the comments in the JS file by adding the @license or @preserve annotation.
>
> /**
>
> * @preserve Copyright 2014 library */

The PrimeFaces Extensions library (or JAR) is configured by default with the Maven resource optimizer. However, you can also configure the Maven resource optimizer plugin for a web project (or WAR).

Once you install the JAR (or WAR) project through the `mvn clean install` command, then the command prompt shows all the CSS and JS files that are going to be optimized, as shown in the following screenshot. This command can also list out the size of the original and optimized resources.

```
[INFO] Optimize CSS file dynaform.css ...
[INFO] Optimize CSS file masterdetail.css ...
[INFO] Optimize CSS file ajaxerrorhandler.css ...
[INFO] Aggregation is running ...
[INFO] 3 files were successfully aggregated.
[INFO] Aggregation is running ...
[INFO] 3 files were successfully aggregated.
[INFO] Optimize JS file core.js ...
[INFO] Optimize JS file ajaxerrorhandler.js ...
[INFO] Optimize JS file spotlight.js ...
[INFO] Optimize JS file widget.js ...
[INFO] Optimize JS file dynaform.js ...
[INFO] Optimize JS file imagerotateandresize.js ...
[INFO] Optimize JS file tristatecheckbox.js ...
[INFO] Optimize JS file tristatemanycheckbox.js ...
[INFO] Aggregation is running ...
[INFO] 8 files were successfully aggregated.
[INFO] Aggregation is running ...
[INFO] 8 files were successfully aggregated.
[INFO] Optimization of resources has been finished successfully.
[INFO] === Statistic =============================================
[INFO] Size of original resources = 1.977 MB
[INFO] Size of optimized resources = 1.341 MB
[INFO] Optimized resources have 67.85% of original size
[INFO] =========================================================
```

# Summary

In this last chapter, you have been introduced to common utility components and Maven plugins to explain the topics such as common utility components and functions to solve problems occurring daily, AjaxErrorHandler for handling the Ajax errors, and Maven resource optimizer plugin for optimizing web resources to improve the web application's performance.

You will now be in a position to know how to use and apply all the new or enhanced PrimeFaces Extensions components into the existing PrimeFaces applications or applications that are developed from scratch. The JobHub application is used to assist you throughout this book with code snippets and screenshots.

The PrimeFaces Extensions team planned to add new components such as the content flow component similar to Apple iTunes, universal select component, new charts component with the chartExporting service, and some more new components with many enhancements to the existing components. As an active open source community project, the PrimeFaces Extensions team encourages the readers to join the community to ask any questions and recommend suggestions to improve the UI library further.

# Index

## Thank you for buying
## Learning PrimeFaces Extensions Development

## About Packt Publishing

Packt, pronounced 'packed', published its first book "*Mastering phpMyAdmin for Effective MySQL Management*" in April 2004 and subsequently continued to specialize in publishing highly focused books on specific technologies and solutions.

Our books and publications share the experiences of your fellow IT professionals in adapting and customizing today's systems, applications, and frameworks. Our solution based books give you the knowledge and power to customize the software and technologies you're using to get the job done. Packt books are more specific and less general than the IT books you have seen in the past. Our unique business model allows us to bring you more focused information, giving you more of what you need to know, and less of what you don't.

Packt is a modern, yet unique publishing company, which focuses on producing quality, cutting-edge books for communities of developers, administrators, and newbies alike. For more information, please visit our website: www.packtpub.com.

## About Packt Open Source

In 2010, Packt launched two new brands, Packt Open Source and Packt Enterprise, in order to continue its focus on specialization. This book is part of the Packt Open Source brand, home to books published on software built around Open Source licences, and offering information to anybody from advanced developers to budding web designers. The Open Source brand also runs Packt's Open Source Royalty Scheme, by which Packt gives a royalty to each Open Source project about whose software a book is sold.

## Writing for Packt

We welcome all inquiries from people who are interested in authoring. Book proposals should be sent to author@packtpub.com. If your book idea is still at an early stage and you would like to discuss it first before writing a formal book proposal, contact us; one of our commissioning editors will get in touch with you.

We're not just looking for published authors; if you have strong technical skills but no writing experience, our experienced editors can help you develop a writing career, or simply get some additional reward for your expertise.

## PrimeFaces Cookbook

ISBN: 978-1-84951-928-1          Paperback: 328 pages

Over 90 practical recipes to learn PrimeFaces - the rapidly evolving, leading JSF component suite

1. The first PrimeFaces book that concentrates on practical approaches rather than the theoretical ones.

2. Readers will gain all the PrimeFaces insights required to complete their JSF projects successfully.

3. Written in a clear, comprehensible style and addresses a wide audience on modern, trend-setting Java/JEE web development.

## Instant PrimeFaces Starter

ISBN: 978-1-84951-990-8          Paperback: 90 pages

Design and develop awesome web user interfaces for desktop and mobile devices with PrimeFaces and JSFz using practical, hands-on examples

1. Learn something new in an Instant! A short, fast, focused guide delivering immediate results.

2. Integrate Google Maps in your web application to show search results with markers and overlays with the PrimeFaces gmap component.

3. Develop a customizable dashboard for your users that displays charts with live data, news feeds, and draggable widgets.

## PrimeFaces Beginner's Guide

ISBN: 978-1-78328-069-8        Paperback: 378 pages

Get your JSF-based projects up and running with this easy-to-implement guide on PrimeFaces

1.  Detailed explanation on how to use basic PrimeFaces UI components like form controls, panels, and layouts.

2.  Delve into PrimeFaces advanced UI Components like Data Tables, menus, charts, file uploading, and themes.

3.  Easy to read and learn with its step-by-step instructions in Time for action and What just happened sections.

## Java EE 6 Development with NetBeans 7

ISBN: 978-1-84951-270-1        Paperback: 392 pages

Develop professional enterprise Java EE applications quickly and easily with this popular IDE

1.  Use features of the popular NetBeans IDE to accelerate development of Java EE applications.

2.  Develop JavaServer Pages (JSPs) to display both static and dynamic content in a web browser.

3.  Covers the latest versions of major Java EE APIs such as JSF 2.0, EJB 3.1, and JPA 2.0, and new additions to Java EE such as CDI and JAX-RS.

4.  Learn development with the popular PrimeFaces JSF 2.0 component library.

Please check **www.PacktPub.com** for information on our titles